Counseling
and
Guilt

RESOURCES FOR
CHRISTIAN COUNSELING

RESOURCES FOR CHRISTIAN COUNSELING

VOLUME EIGHT

Counseling
and
Guilt

EARL D. WILSON, Ph.D.

RESOURCES FOR
CHRISTIAN COUNSELING

───── General Editor ─────

Gary R. Collins, Ph.D.

WORD PUBLISHING
Dallas · London · Sydney · Singapore

Library of Congress Cataloging-in-Publication Data

Wilson, Earl D., 1939–
    Counseling and guilt.

    (Resources for Christian counseling ; v. 8)
    Bibliography: p.
    Includes index.
    1. Guilt—Religious aspects—Christianity.
2. Pastoral counseling. I. Title. II. Series.
BT722.W55 1987   253.5   87-8258
ISBN 0-8499-0591-5

Printed in the United States of America

    239   AGF   98765

CONTENTS

EDITOR'S PREFACE

SEVERAL MONTHS AGO I had an opportunity to visit the Viet Nam war memorial in Washington, D. C. I had read about this controversial monument and seen many pictures, but I was not prepared for my emotional response to the monument. Viet Nam had always seemed far away and I know only a few people who fought in that war. Even so, the statue of those three tense, tired soldiers and the massive granite wall engraved with the names of the dead were very moving. Even more moving were the flowers, little flags, mementos, and families staring at the name of some loved one who had died, sometimes barely out of adolescence.

My visit helped me to understand why Admiral Zumwalt, the man who commanded naval operations for a part of the war, still, at the time of this writing, has not been able to visit the memorial. The scene brings back memories that he and many others must find too painful to contemplate.

In other countries and other parts of the world, the memorials are different, but the pain can be equally severe. For Americans, the Viet Nam War ended over a decade ago, but many veterans and their families still struggle with the physical and psychological pain left over from those difficult days in their country's history. Counselors still work actively with veterans who only now are coming to terms with their stresses and emotional reactions to the war.

One of the emotional reactions is guilt. "These veterans don't need counselors," one psychologist wrote in a professional journal. "They are more in need of pastors who can help them deal with guilt and find forgiveness."

There are times when this could apply to all of us. It is easy to feel like David whose strength and health slipped away when he tried to hide his sin and stifle his guilt. Relief came only when he faced his sin honestly and said "I will confess my transgressions unto the Lord." It was then that he felt the weight of guilt fall from his shoulders and experienced the joy of sins forgiven (Psalm 32:5).

When the people at Word Books approached me about editing a series of books on counseling, I knew that many of the volumes would have to deal with current issues like eating disorders, family abuse, infertility, and abortion. But no counseling series would be complete without a fresh look at those topics that are centuries old—but as up-to-date as this morning's newspaper. Guilt is one of those core topics.

The Resources for Christian Counseling is a series of books dealing with topics, old and new, that are likely to come up in your counseling. Written by counseling experts, each of whom has a strong Christian commitment and practical counseling experience, these volumes are intended to be examples of accurate psychology and careful use of Scripture. Each is intended to have a clear evangelical perspective, careful documentation, a strong practical orientation, and freedom from the sweeping statements and undocumented rhetoric that sometimes characterize books in the counseling field. Our goal is to provide books that are clearly written, practical, up-to-date overviews of the issues faced by contemporary Christian counselors. All of the Resources for Christian Counseling books have similar bindings and together they will comprise a complete encyclopedia of Christian counseling.

In some way, most of the topics discussed in this series deal indirectly with guilt. This volume by Earl Wilson focuses on guilt directly. It is written by a man who is well qualified for the task in terms of training and experience. Dr. Wilson is a professional counselor with a doctorate in psychology. He is a committed Christian, a respected public speaker, a seminary professor, and author of several previous and highly-acclaimed books on counseling.

The following pages are intended to increase your understanding of guilt and help you counsel effectively with those who are guilty or who feel guilty (these aren't always the same). The author's conclusions can apply to those Viet Nam veterans who still have moral struggles about their months in southeast Asia. But the book will apply even more to the people who come to you for help with their problems of guilt. Unlike most other books on this topic, the last chapter discusses the significant but often overlooked issue of guilt in the counselor.

Over the years, I have read numerous books and perhaps dozens of articles on guilt. Even with this background, I have been helped by Dr. Wilson in my understanding of this significant and foundational counseling issue. I hope the following pages will be used by God to enable you to help others deal with guilt and find the forgiveness that comes only in Christ.

Gary R. Collins, Ph.D.
Kildeer, Illinois

INTRODUCTION

GUILT—SUCH A SIMPLE WORD. Common and familiar. We usually feel comfortable with familiar words and phrases. They give us a sense of mastery. *Counseling* with guilt. How does that sound? The familiarity is there. It is a common experience. As Christians involved in counseling we encounter guilt-ridden persons daily. What about the sense of mastery? Has practice made perfect?

My colleague shared his thoughts on the subject quite forcefully. "I'll never get used to it," he said. "There is no box big enough to hold all the persons with guilt. They represent a mammoth challenge for the counselor. They are all unique and need to be seen as individuals. It is not an easy task."

The simple, familiar topic, counseling with guilt, becomes complex and baffling when it is moved from the nondescript, academic status of a book or a classroom into the personal confines of the counseling office. In this volume we will attempt to deal with the complexities of guilt and provide a framework for understanding the problems of the individual client. The reader is encouraged to develop and maintain an individual mindset. He or she should seek to keep in mind the uniqueness of each guilt-ridden person with whom counseling is done. This approach may be somewhat foreign because we often use problem categories, such as guilt, to group people so that we then can present generalized solutions.

There are solutions for persons who struggle with guilt and there are some answers in this volume. There are also principles and techniques which the counselor must evaluate and try in order to increase his or her repertoire of personal skills. Practice will be needed in order to select and perfect those distinctions and skills which will give the counselor confidence in working with guilt. In that regard, the book is designed to be read and studied while working with counselees.

The author is indebted to numerous colleagues and students who have commented on many of the ideas presented. Their insights have been most helpful for the continued development of these ideas. Especially do I single out my psychology students at Western Conservative Baptist Seminary who have been both patient and insightful as I have presented in class a number of the concepts found in this volume.

I am also indebted to the men and women who have come to me for counseling and who have shared their struggles with guilt with me in the professional setting. Many of their stories are used as illustrations in this book. The identities of these persons have been carefully protected by disguising the stories and, in some cases, by bringing two or three people together in one example. They shared their lives with me as a valued trust and I have worked hard to show the respect they deserve while at the same time enriching the readers' experience by including their unique insights.

I would be remiss in not drawing attention to the tremendous contribution that my wife and children have made to this particular content. Families produce guilt and families also ameliorate guilt. I praise God for my wife Sandy, and our children—Marci, Mark, Mike, Melissa, Michelle, and John—who have loved me despite the fact that this writing stood in the way of my having time with them. Thanks, Gang!

I am also appreciative of the way my family allows me to share their lives in both written and spoken form. I have not violated their confidences. They have agreed to participate with me in my ministry by sharing some of their stories, and I am richer—and you will be richer—because of this openness. Finally, I want to acknowledge the helpful spirit and personal competence extended to me by Gary Collins. He uniquely combines the gifts of encouragement and exhortation which make him a fine general editor.

What is your objective in reading this volume? How will you know whether or not it has been worthwhile? I use visual pictures in my mind to help me answer such questions. Allow me to share my visual for you. I envision a peaceful look on your face as you watch a couple leave your office arm in arm. They smile for the first time in months because they have been released from their guilt and united again in their love. May our gracious God use the insights provided here to accomplish that end.

Counseling
and
Guilt

RESOURCES FOR
CHRISTIAN COUNSELING

PART ONE

UNDERSTANDING GUILT

CHAPTER ONE

THE CHALLENGES OF COUNSELING
FOR GUILT

"Working with people's guilt mystifies me," said an experienced psychotherapist. "I can't seem to find an effective way to help the many people I see who suffer with this problem. Sometimes I try to act like it isn't real, but it doesn't go away. Or, I point out that it is a problem with the client's value system, but that still does not take it away. I feel very frustrated."

HOW DOES GUILT AFFECT US?

Pastors and counselors cannot ignore guilt. They must deal with it every day. Sometimes people are bothered by their guilt, other times they are not. Sometimes counselees have tried to deal with the guilt, other times they have not.

Jim was suffering from severe abdominal pain when he first came to the counseling center. He had seen his family doctor and an internal medicine specialist. Neither could diagnose his problem. After several hours of guarded self-disclosure Jim began to go deeper into himself. He told the counselor about a period of his life that he had never shared with anyone before. He spoke of the emotional energy it took to keep the secrets. He related how he had wanted to talk to God about his shame but that he had felt not even God could forgive or understand.

"When the pains in my stomach started," Jim said, "I just knew that I was under a curse. I was sure I had stomach cancer and I thought it was God's way of punishing me. I put off dealing with the guilt for two years just hoping it would go away or that I would die."

Mary's situation was much different. She came from a fine Christian home with strict moral standards. She violated those standards after she was engaged, and became pregnant.

"I feel like a part of me has died," she said. "I don't think I will ever be able to look my family in the face again."

Fortunately for Mary she went to a counselor who helped her face herself and her family. With his help she made some good decisions and began to get her life back in order. Receiving God's forgiveness was easier once she got things straightened out with her family.

Susan was brought to the counseling center after having cried uncontrollably for several days.

"I don't know what's wrong with me," she blurted out between sobs. "I've never been like this before."

The counselor was patient and gave Susan a chance to take a good look at herself.

"Why do I feel so guilty?" Susan asked one day. "I really haven't done anything wrong. I keep feeling like I must be letting everyone down and when I feel that way I just can't control the tears. I'm such a mess and, yes, I even feel guilty about that."

The counselor helped Susan make a distinction between guilt and disappointment. Once Susan could deal with disappointment over not meeting her own expectations she was on the way to tear-free days.

Pete was an alcoholic who was practically dragged to the counseling center under the threat of divorce. For weeks he denied his problem. It was always someone else's fault. Sure, he drank a little but it was nothing he couldn't control. He could take it or leave it. After a time the counselor finally got through to Pete and he realized that he was not in control of his life. He voluntarily went through an alcohol treatment program and stopped drinking. Once Pete stopped "self-medicating" he was ready to explore some of the roots of his drinking problem. Three things stood out—fear, feelings of inferiority, and guilt. Pete went from total denial to vicious self-blame. He could trace his self-punishment back to his early childhood and he realized that even at the age of six he had felt the burden of never being good enough and always feeling guilty.

These glimpses into four lives only begin to scratch the surface of the ways in which guilt affects people's lives. Suicide, eating disorders, crime, workaholism, broken marriages, drug abuse, even gossip and rigid legalism—all tell the story of guilt. The problem is indeed a large one.

David Augsburger writes:

> Guilt, with all its complexities, is a terrifying foe for any man. Trying to identify it is somewhat like wrestling an octopus in a darkened aquarium at midnight.[1]

What Is Guilt?

Most dictionaries define guilt as a feeling of shame or remorse. It is the subjective reaction of persons to some of their thoughts or behavior. Persons experiencing guilt are self-critical and self-condemning. They have put themselves under the burden of their own self-judgments and what they consider to be the judgments of society. Life for them seems to be a private prison from which there appears to be no escape.

There is another side to guilt: the legal side. A judge or jury pronounces an offender guilty. Such a pronouncement carries with it a penalty or a sentence. It doesn't really matter how the person feels about what he or she has done; the verdict is "guilty as charged" and the consequences must be paid. Matters of motivation are not always taken into account. A law has been broken and a penalty must be paid.

Not all those who are legally guilty experience guilt. Therefore, the possibility exists that those who experience feelings of guilt are not guilty, while those who do not feel guilty are indeed legally guilty. Counselors are often asked to deal with both types of persons. Patience and careful discernment are required to help individuals work through their confusion in these areas.

Guilt may take on another dimension when viewed from a counseling perspective. Guilt can become a personality trait or a prevailing mood. It is for some a way of life that must be challenged and corrected if the counselee is to reach his or her full potential.

Jane said, "There isn't a minute that goes by that I don't blame myself for something. If I haven't done something wrong I will probably dredge up something from the past."

It is clear that some of Jane's feelings of shame may be based in objective reality. She has done some wrong things. She feels guilty because she *is* guilty. On the other hand she may experience similar feelings when her behavior is not wrong, inappropriate, or sinful. She may experience guilt because she has judged herself for outcomes that are outside her control. Disappointment may be felt as feelings of guilt or inadequacy, but all of these situations are interpreted by Jane in the same way. She feels guilty.

The counselor's job is to help her sort out the myriad of thoughts and feelings which she may have so that she can gain relief from either her actions or her interpretation of her actions. She may need forgiveness or she may need to make restitution. On the other hand, she may need to reset her expectations for herself or she may need to be released from the expectations of others. From Jane's initial perspective it may all look the same. It is up to the pastor or her counselor to help her bring understanding to her chaotic world. Without such help she may continue with these unresolved feelings until they eventually destroy her.

THE CHALLENGES OF COUNSELING WITH GUILT

Why set guilt apart as a special topic for the counselor? Because working with guilt offers several specific challenges that the counselor must meet.

First is the dual challenge of *understanding and acceptance.* This challenge is not unique to working with guilt. In fact, it is the challenge of counseling itself. To be effective the counselor must establish a basis of communication with the counselee. This is begun by listening, but not the level of listening to which we are accustomed. Most listening involves attending to the person only until enough is heard to enable the hearer to give an articulate response. The talker in such interactions becomes aware that he or she has been tuned out halfway through the conversation and sometimes feels misunderstood. In contrast, the effective counselor listens to get to know as much as can be known about the counselee. People are flattered and encouraged to talk when they feel someone really wants to know them. When listening is inadequate they feel misunderstood and guilt is increased rather than lessened. Counseling without understanding becomes part of the problem rather than part of the solution.

Coupled with the need to understand is the need to communicate acceptance of the person. Please note that I said "acceptance of the person" not acceptance of the behavior which may be at the heart of the guilt. Acceptance is important because most people who suffer from guilt suffer in silence. They believe that they are so bad that if people knew them they would not accept them. Guilt-ridden people are usually very sensitive to rejection, even when it is subtle.

The counselor communicates acceptance best by careful listening. You show them that they have value because you take the time to understand and to really get to know them as people. You also serve them by accepting them as people and providing them with a base for challenging their beliefs that people would not accept them if they really knew.

When asked by a friend how his first counseling session had gone, Don flashed a smile and said, "Fine—I felt understood for the first time and I also felt accepted. I think there is hope."

The second challenge of counseling with guilt is the need to *analyze the problem*. As was shown earlier, not all feelings of shame or remorse come from the same source. Psychologists have categorized guilt in several ways as will be discussed later. Suffice it to say at this point that the counselor must distinguish between five or six different types of guilt that may be affecting the counselee. In some cases the counselee does not even realize that his or her uncomfortable feelings are rooted in guilt. Some guilt may be earned, other unearned, but the feelings of the counselee may be the same. It is up to the counselor to help persons understand themselves enough to begin to work toward a solution to the problem. I have found that once clients can understand the source of their guilty feelings they can be helped to deal with them in the most complete manner.

This leads to the next challenge: *to help counselees get beyond their guilt so that their lives can be restored to some semblance of hope and peace.* It is the counselor's job to help the person find forgiveness or other relief from the problem and thus allow hope to return. Sometimes this is most difficult because you are dealing with feelings that may continually reoccur. Many counselees have become almost obsessed with their guilt. After we have considered the nature and causes of guilt, Part Two of this volume will focus in detail upon intervention strategies to help persons move beyond their guilt.

Jesus instructed people to go and sin no more. This is often difficult for those who are burdened with guilt, because their sin is carried with them wherever they go. It is an internal problem and therefore may require both outward steps, such as asking for forgiveness from another, and inward steps, such as forgiving self.

The next challenge in working with guilt comes in the form of a warning. *Avoid quick solutions.* Problems of guilt are rarely helped by injunctions or pat answers. In fact, most pat answers leave the person feeling even more guilty than before.

When Greg talked to his pastor about his feelings of guilt he was told that God had forgiven him and that he shouldn't worry about it any more. "Just trust the Lord" was the pastoral counselor's short remark as Greg walked out the door.

"Okay," Greg replied.

But it wasn't really okay. As he drove away from the church he began to berate himself for his lack of faith. Now he had a new source of guilt. He felt guilty for not trusting the Lord. Greg would have received more help if his counselor had avoided the pat answers and taken some time to teach him in a practical way what it means to trust the Lord. A few examples would have gone a long way.

A final challenge in working with persons who suffer with guilt is the challenge of *multiple problems.* Although guilt may be the focal problem for a person, it rarely occurs by itself. It may be accompanied by such conditions as anger, depression, physical complaints, social inadequacies, substance abuse, or even psychosis. In such instances the counselor needs to deal with the entire problem, not just the symptom or the cause. When a person has dealt with the guilt, the habits that have been formed in reaction to the guilt may persist. These unwanted conditions must be dealt with or the person will experience self-doubt and eventually new guilt because the maladaptive habits have not gone away.

I have discovered that many persons have been done a disservice because when some of their symptoms persist after the guilt has been addressed they are told they must not really have asked God to forgive them. The counselor has become the judge and not the servant. This undermines their sense of self-confidence and often their belief in God. How much better to say, "Now that the repentance and forgiveness issues have been taken care of, let's work on the maladaptive habits or the other feelings that have developed with the guilt."

UNDERSTANDING THE IMPACT

We have seen then that the effects of guilt are widespread and that guilt may manifest itself in many different ways in the counselees we serve. Effective counseling with guilt requires patience, sensitivity, and a willingness to listen. Appropriate intervention strategies can be learned, but they must be built upon an attitude of prayer. I have found it helpful to distinguish between guilty persons and persons with guilt.

God longs to forgive sin and take away the guilt. In that sense repentant persons are not guilty persons. They may, however, still be persons with guilt. As counselors, we have the privilege of helping them work through those feelings to a place of new freedom and hope in their lives.

CHAPTER TWO

BIBLICAL PERSPECTIVES ON GUILT

WHEN WE APPROACH THE PROBLEM OF GUILT we are considering a counseling problem that is directly addressed by God's Word. Guilt is a theological as well as a psychological problem; therefore, understanding the biblical perspective is vital to relevant counseling in this area.

In Proverbs we read the following words:

A man tormented by the guilt of murder will be a fugitive till death; let no one support him.   (Prov. 28:17)

Although this Scripture focuses upon a severe crime, murder, the effects of guilt are just as common with sins less sensational. This verse highlights both the psychological aspects of guilt, such as torment, and the legal aspects, addressed by the idea of "fugitive" or one hiding from the law. The phrase "let no one support him" suggests that the man was impenitent and that others were not to assist him in his flight from God, from the law, or from himself. As long as a man is fleeing from God there is no relief from the torment of guilt. As long as a man chooses to stay in the fugitive status he will not find relief from guilt. From the biblical perspective there is no relief without the satisfaction of the demands of a righteous God. This point is softened, however, when we realize that God has gone out of his way to be satisfied. He even arranged for the payment of his own penalty. That is what the gospel is all about.

How Does God Use Guilt?

There has been much confusion within the church as to the role of guilt in the way that God relates to people. In the book of Leviticus God instituted the guilt offering. It was a sacrifice for sin much like the sin offering and the burnt offering.

Several aspects of this offering are interesting in terms of our consideration of guilt. First, it covered unintentional as well as deliberate sins. Second, it required restitution, and, third, it carried with it the repeated promise of forgiveness.

And as a penalty he must bring to the priest, that is, to the Lord, his guilt offering, a ram from the flock, one without defect and of the proper value. In this way the priest will make atonement for him before the Lord, and he will be forgiven for any of these things he did that made him guilty. (Lev. 6:6, 7)

It is clear that God is not soft on sin. He required both a restitution and a sacrifice. It is also clear that God did not desire to punish humans with guilt. The wages of sin is death, not guilt. Since God does not change, we can be sure he does not intend to inflict a punishment of guilt upon humans today. The same sacrifice necessary to pay the penalty for sin is intended to remove the guilt as well. This passage teaches that God desires that we be totally freed from guilt. This raises several new questions about the purpose of guilt.

Is Guilt Necessary for Salvation?

We are told in the Gospel of John that one of the works of the Holy Spirit is to bring conviction regarding sin, righteousness, and judgment.

> When he comes, he will convict the world of guilt in regard to sin and righteousness and judgment: in regard to sin, because men do not believe in me; in regard to righteousness, because I am going to the Father, where you can see me no longer; and in regard to judgment, because the prince of this world now stands condemned.
>
> (John 16:8–11)

Although the translators of the New International Version cited above chose to use the phrase, "convict the world of guilt" the word *guilt* does not appear in the Greek text. The word which is used for "convict" is the word *elengkhō* which means "to admonish, convict, convince, tell a fault, rebuke, or repent." The passage could be reworded "establish a conviction" of sin, righteousness, and judgment. The Revised Standard Version uses the simple word "convince."

The key issue, recognition of sin and separation from God, may or may not carry with it strong feelings of remorse, the emotional aspect of guilt. It seems clear, however, that without a recognition of the legal aspects of guilt, accepting God's verdict about our sin, a person would not go to him for salvation. Thus the purpose of the law as stated in Romans 3:19:

> Now we know that whatever the law says, it says to those who are under the law, so that every mouth may be silenced and the whole world held accountable to God.

Repentance, seeing our sin as God sees it, is necessary for salvation. But, depending on the individual, the act of repentance may be accompanied by a strong wave of remorse or a simple intellectual acknowledgment of the fact that the person has missed the mark and needs God.

Thus the answer to our question is both yes and no. Guilt is necessary for salvation; but then again, it isn't. The legal aspect of guilt, acknowledging sin and accepting God's payment, is necessary for salvation while the emotional remorseful aspect may not play such an important role. Just trying to bring people to feel badly about their sin may not result in salvation. The Holy Spirit works to bring conviction through our minds as well as our emotions. Conviction of sin is a belief about our actions, not just a feeling of goodness or badness. Thus, the cause of Christ may best be served by careful teaching about the perfection of God and the absoluteness of his requirements for salvation rather than focusing upon and trying to create feelings which may lead to remorse or despair and miss true repentance.

Is Guilt a Necessary Condition for Continued Christian Growth?

In some Christian circles it is either stated or implied that if you don't feel guilty or remorseful you must not be growing as a Christian. The implication is that as you look to God in all his splendor you feel remorseful about yourself and thus you are motivated to grow. I believe this view is false. As I stated in *The Discovered Self*, the anchor-point of our self-esteem is God and we grow as we elevate him, not when we lower ourselves or cripple ourselves by holding onto guilt over sin for which Christ died to free us.

God's forgiveness and acceptance is an anchor-point for resolving the identity crisis because it gives us a place to go. Without forgiveness life is a dead-end street. Regardless of the path we take, we always end up at a place in our lives from which there is no place to go. We are locked in by our sin and our human limitations. God opens the door and ushers us into new, often unexplored, territory. Who am I? I am an explorer. I am free to make an impact upon my world. I have been given not only the opportunity, but also the responsibility to make a difference. Because God frees me from the limitations of my sin, I am up to the task—not fully prepared, but ready to be prepared as I go along.[1]

28

You and I will not grow if we are not sensitive to sin. But we also will not grow unless we focus on the Savior rather than our sin. The writer of the book of Hebrews puts this whole issue in proper perspective.

> Therefore, since we are surrounded by such a great cloud of witnesses, let us throw off everything that hinders and the sin that so easily entangles, and let us run with perseverance the race marked out for us. Let us fix our eyes on Jesus, the author and perfecter of our faith, who for the joy set before him endured the cross, scorning its shame, and sat down at the right hand of the throne of God.
>
> (Heb. 12:1, 2)

There is no attempt to motivate by guilt in these verses. The emphasis is clear. Throw off sin, look at the Savior, run the race. Guilt-ridden people have trouble fixing their eyes on Jesus. In fact, helping people look at Jesus and not at their sin is one of the most productive ways of helping them work through guilt. Solid growth comes from eating sound food, not from bemoaning their intake of junk.

Peter wrote,

> But grow in the grace and knowledge of our Lord and Savior Jesus Christ. To him be glory both now and forever!
>
> (2 Pet. 3:18)

The knowledge of the Lord Jesus Christ promotes growth. The phrase, "grow in grace," suggests an important alternative to focusing upon our guilt. God's unmerited favor is available to sinners and it energizes. Focusing on sin depresses and kills the spirit.

Is Guilt Necessary to Prevent Pride?

Solomon highlighted the dangers of pride with this strong but simple statement:

> Pride goes before destruction, a haughty spirit before a fall.   (Prov. 16:18)

29

Fear of pride, like other fears, often leads people to react in some strange ways. Joe was so afraid of pride that he often flagellated himself over past sin. He kept his remorse alive in the hope that there would be no fertile soil left in which pride could grow. The plan backfired, however, because he reached the point where he became proud of his asceticism.

We joke about becoming proud of our humility but for some people this is a reality. When people focus upon sin in order to remain humble they are not following God's plan. In fact, guilt-ridden people often fall into pride as a means of supporting their sagging egos. People were not made to wallow in sin and therefore may become proud in other areas to make up for their deficits. If guilt does not prevent pride, what is the answer to the problem of pride? I believe the book of Philippians has the answer. We are told to imitate the humility shown by Jesus Christ.

> Your attitude should be the same as that of Christ Jesus.
> (Phil. 2:5)

The key to humility in the life of Christ was obedience. He was without sin and therefore guilt was not a possibility. Obedience will keep us from pride, especially the kind of obedience Jesus modeled which placed the will of God and the needs of mankind ahead of personal desires. Absence of pride does not mean that you devalue yourself. It only means that you are not to think of yourself more highly than you should (see Romans 12:3).

Peter emphasizes submissiveness as a key to humility.

> Young men, in the same way be submissive to those who are older. Clothe yourselves with humility toward one another, because, "God opposes the proud but gives grace to the humble." Humble yourselves, therefore, under God's mighty hand, that he may lift you up in due time. Cast all your anxiety on him because he cares for you. (1 Pet. 5:5-7)

Guilt tends to produce withdrawal from people. It also leads to self-centered activity that is not compatible with submissiveness or humility. Mindy said, "The more I tried to cover up my guilt the more arrogant I became. It was like I was trying to make up for my mistakes by being better than everyone else."

Scripture is quite clear in emphasizing that comparisons with other people are a major source of pride. Notice this statement: Each one should test his own actions. Then he can take pride in himself, without comparing himself to somebody else" (Gal. 6:4). We are not told to devalue our actions or to feel guilty for our failures—we are simply told not to compare.

God has many ways of keeping us humble. I don't believe that guilt is the primary way to do it. Usually I am most humbled when I look at his great attributes, not my inabilities or my sin. When I see who he is I want to submit to him.

I do not believe guilt is necessary to prevent pride. In fact, I would argue that where guilt is overemphasized people may struggle with pride as a means of overcompensating for the remorse that they feel. The answer to pride is to get people's eyes off of themselves and their sin and onto Jesus Christ. He, not guilt, is the pathway to humility.

Does Guilt Prevent Future Sin?

Many people fear that if they forget their past sin they will be more vulnerable to future sin. Most of these people believe that taking sin lightly is a serious mistake. But is guilt necessary to avoid taking sin lightly? I do not believe so.

We can recognize the dangers of sin without wasting time and valuable spiritual and emotional energy punishing ourselves over actions for which God has already forgiven us. I believe it is just as easy to quench the Spirit by reliving the past sin as it is by committing new sin. In either case the individual is denying the power of God, choosing rather to think more about sin than about the Savior.

When guilt is used as a form of self-punishment it has the same effect as other punishments. It only suppresses other behavior. As soon as the guilt is removed the suppressed behavior will occur. If those who are tempted try to deal with the temptation by focusing on guilt they will often indulge themselves in the sin to "make themselves feel better."

Jerry's life is a good example of this problem. He repeatedly tells himself how bad he is because of his sexual thoughts. If he succeeds in making himself feel bad enough he will end up going to an adult bookstore to view pornography. When asked why, he says, "I just felt so bad I couldn't stop. I knew it would occupy my mind for a while and make me feel better."

In other cases, as soon as the guilt slackens the suppressed sin will occur. Marge's problem with drinking illustrates this phenomenon. She said, "I always get drunk when I feel better. I stay dry as long as I can feel guilty about being a drunk. When something good happens I forget and then I drink. I need a positive plan. Trying to stay guilty hasn't worked."

Another reason why guilt does not work as a deterrent to sin is that it requires such an expenditure of emotional and spiritual energy. The energy and effort needed to resist temptation is used up by dealing with the guilt. Bill said, "I'm totally exhausted. I don't even feel like I can fight sin anymore. I spend everything I have trying to get relief from my guilt."

God has chosen to give us the power to remember our past. We remember our sins. God is the only one who forgets sin (see Isaiah 43:25). I believe, however, that God, in giving us memories, did not intend so much that we remember our sins, but that we remember how vulnerable we are to sin. When we know that God has forgotten our sin we also know that we are no longer under the guilt that comes because of the burden of that sin. It is wise to realize our need to depend upon God to help us resist sin. Guilt-ridden people do not depend on God very well because they are often afraid to come boldly before the throne of grace (Heb. 4:16). Sin is best countered by remembering the goodness of God and forming a strong desire to please God, not in remembering our guilt and then trying to coddle ourselves.

No temptation has seized you except what is common to man. And God is faithful; he will not let you be tempted beyond what you can bear. But when you are tempted, he will also provide a way out so that you can stand up under it.   (1 Cor. 10:13)

This is a great promise from a God whom we can count upon. It is always better to trust in God to prevent future sin, than to trust in guilt.

Does Guilt Help Keep Sin in Perspective?

Janet's father was very concerned about his daughter's Christian life. He wanted to train her in the way she should go. His desire was that she be a sensitive, responsible believer. He tried to accomplish this by reminding her of her sins and implying that she should feel guilty for her imperfections. He believed that if he reminded Janet of her sin she would feel guilty and thus remain sensitive to sin. But his method failed and so did Janet.

She reached the point where she did not really consider the issues her dad was raising because they were covered with an overlay of guilt. She spent all of her energies focusing on the guilt and did not really attend to his instruction. This is illustrated in the figures below:

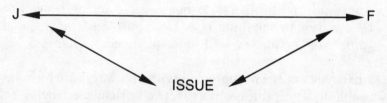

ISSUE

Open Communication, Issues are Considered

In this figure we see the normal father-daughter communication. Father is free to bring up an issue, for example, breaking curfew, and Janet is able to consider it and give her father an explanation. Janet may also introduce issues for her father to consider. Now, notice what happens when you add an overlay of guilt to the situation (see p. 34). Guilt, or the promoting of feelings of guilt, breaks the direct communication line between Janet and her father and also confuses the original issue so that it is not dealt with adequately, if at all.

Father still has the original issue which Janet will not consider. This spins off into a new, even more emotional, issue (**A**), for father, Janet's irresponsibility. On the other side Janet will

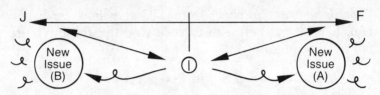

Communication Shattered by Guilt

also develop a new issue (B), feelings of being attacked by Father. Effective communication is impossible as long as this process is not corrected. In fact, it usually progresses geometrically. Guilt is applied to the new issues and this spins off to issue after issue, all of which are never addressed until the relationship has been totally destroyed. I have observed literally hundreds of relationships that have been destroyed by this process. An alternative must be found if disaster is to be averted.

Scripture emphasizes straight talk, not guilt talk.

> Above all, my brothers, do not swear—not by heaven or by earth or by anything else. Let your "Yes" be yes, and your "No," no, or you will be condemned.   (James 5:12)

I have always been impressed with the ways in which Jesus was able to bring sin into perspective without destroying relationships. When he spoke with the sinful woman at the well he asked questions that got to the issue of her sin. He led her to discover her sin and her need of salvation, but he did not attack her with guilt. This beautiful conversation ends with the woman looking for the Messiah and Jesus revealing that he is the Messiah.

> The woman said, "I know that Messiah (called Christ) is coming. When he comes, he will explain everything to us." Then Jesus declared, "I who speak to you am he."
> (John 4:25, 26)

The conviction of sin is there but the relationship was not hindered or sidetracked by guilt. She got the message. Guilt may

result from facts, but when the emphasis is placed on producing guilt the facts of sin may be ignored. After pointing out the
facts of sin Jesus did not say, "Go and feel guilty." He said,
"Go and sin no more."

DAVID'S PERSPECTIVE ON SIN AND GUILT

Of all the sinners mentioned in the Bible one would expect
David to have struggled with guilt. He was a very sensitive
man, yet he became insensitive to God and persons around
him. This resulted in premeditated adultery and murder. We
might expect these kinds of sin to haunt him the rest of his life.

David did in fact go through some real periods of remorse
and soul-searching repentance as is evidenced in Psalm 51. He
was a broken man. But he did not stay broken. He was lifted
up by God to a new place of fellowship and a new place of
serving God. What was his secret? What did he know that can
help you and me move forward after sin threatens to destroy
us? I believe the answers are found in Psalm 32:4, 5.

> For day and night your hand was heavy upon me; my
> strength was sapped as in the heat of summer. Then I ac-
> knowledged my sin to you and did not cover up my iniq-
> uity. I said, "I will confess my transgression to the
> Lord"—and you forgave the guilt of my sin.

David's remorse regarding his sin even sapped his physical
strength. His response was to go back to God and start over.
He held nothing back. He acknowledged it all. God's response
was not only to forgive the transgressions but also to deal with
the guilt. David did not hold onto his remorse. He let God take
it also. Is it any wonder he was able to proclaim,

> You are my hiding place; you will protect me from trouble
> and surround me with songs of deliverance. (Psalm 32:7)

God was not through dealing with David's sin until he had
restored him to a complete place of blessing. This included the
removal of his guilt. God restored David in terms of both the
legal and the emotional aspects of guilt. He was truly forgiven,

and he accepted the full range of restoration. Restoration cannot take place until the crippling aspects of guilt are gone.

BIBLICAL "BOTTOM LINES" REGARDING GUILT

Although Scripture does not say everything that could be said about guilt it says all that we really need to know. There are several bottom-line conclusions that can be drawn. These conclusions can serve as a base for personal healing and for ministry to those who struggle with guilt.

First, *guilt is a reality.* We feel guilty because we are guilty. Our sin has separated us from God. We have broken God's laws. James states:

> For whoever keeps the whole law and yet stumbles at just one point is guilty of breaking all of it.   (James 2:10)

Second, *God does not intend that we remain under the curse of guilt.* He has chosen to release us from the penalty of our sin because Christ has paid the penalty for us. He also desires to release us from the guilt of our sin. I believe that the promise of John chapter 8 also applies to freedom from guilt.

> Jesus replied, "I tell you the truth, everyone who sins is a slave to sin. Now a slave has no permanent place in the family, but a son belongs to it forever. So if the Son sets you free, you will be free indeed.   (John 8:34–36)

Third, *humans tend toward evil and prefer to ponder evil rather than good.* One of the results of pondering evil is to remain under the curse of guilt.

> The heart is deceitful above all things and beyond cure. Who can understand it? "I the Lord search the heart and examine the mind, to reward a man according to his conduct, according to what his deeds deserve." (Jer. 17:9, 10)

We play with guilt under the guise that it is keeping us from sin when in reality it is making us more vulnerable to the evil one. It is just as dangerous to ponder sin after it has been forgiven as it is to play with it until it happens.

Finally, *guilt feelings and personal behavior must be evaluated in terms of the teachings of Scripture.* Only as persons examine themselves and compare their behavior with the teachings of Scripture are they able to determine whether or not God's laws have been violated. David was free from guilt and was able to invite God to examine him.

Test me, O Lord, and try me, examine my heart and my mind. (Psalm 26:2)

In the New Testament we are instructed regarding self-examination in both the context of sin and the context of our work for God. In giving instruction regarding the Lord's Supper, Paul calls for self-examination:

A man ought to examine himself before he eats of the bread and drinks of the cup. (1 Cor. 11:28)

We are to take communion with a clear conscience so that we will not make a mockery of the body and blood of Christ. On the other hand, we are able to receive the glorious message of the Lord's Supper in all of its beauty when we have been fully cleansed from our guilt.

In Galatians Paul challenges us to test our works. A part of evaluating works is to realize that we have given ourselves to God and that he has chosen to bless us. This type of examination also tends to free us from guilt.

Each one should test his own actions. Then he can take pride in himself, without comparing himself to somebody else, for each one should carry his own load. (Gal. 6:4, 5)

Some of the most important work we as counselors can do to help persons who suffer from guilt is to teach them the truth of Scripture concerning their guilt. They need to be free and the biblical perspective can bring them to the truth that guilt is only a virtue if it leads to repentance and newness of relationship with Christ. After that it usually serves no godly purpose.

CHAPTER THREE

PSYCHOLOGICAL PERSPECTIVES
ON GUILT

COUNSELORS HAVE BEEN STYMIED FOR CENTURIES in treating problems of guilt. The treatment of guilt is very time-consuming and the counselor often doesn't know what to do with or for the counselee. No chemical treatments are available which treat guilt directly and no verbal therapies have proven to be especially effective. The fact is there is no psychological cure for a condition that exists in a high percentage of all psychological problems.

Karl Menninger has highlighted the issue.

. . . the crying needs of millions of people—disturbed, miserable, angry, depressed, often deluded, and guilt-laden people—continued to go untended. Not that some colleagues did not hear these cries and do their best to respond with services and counsel. But the help was quantitatively inconspicuous compared to the visible need, and the "psychotherapy" remedy was seen as obviously inadequate to the now apparent task.[1]

WHAT ARE THE OPTIONS?

If there are no biochemical treatments for guilt and there are no specific psychological cures, then what options are there from the psychological perspective?

The response of the late fifties and early sixties was to work on *stamping out the source of guilt.* Convince people that they should not feel guilty. Help them to come to believe that there is nothing wrong with violating family standards. Point out, for example, that abortion or divorce is legal and that it is their right. Desensitize them to those things that result in feelings of guilt. In other words, work on the outside structure and people's view of it. Create for the counselee an interpretation of the world that allows for the behavior that is producing those feelings of guilt. Do away with the conscience, which is an unneeded vestige of infantile experience.

Another option, presented by the human potential movement in the late sixties and seventies, was *"up with the person."* Counselees were encouraged to see themselves as more than their guilt. The cry was: Realize your full potential for good and you will overcome your beliefs that you are a failure and that you should feel guilty. This boot-strap approach was very helpful to many people, especially for those whose guilt was unfounded. For others it dissolved into a "think happy thoughts" situation. Present failures raised serious doubts about the resolution of past failures and the fear and guilt returned. People were encouraged to return to seeing the good in themselves. Some made it and some didn't. The underlying issues and notions of wrongdoing were not really addressed.

A third option was to concentrate on the *fear-of-punishment* aspect of guilt. Avoid punishment at all costs. "You are only guilty if you get caught," we were told. "No one knows and they won't know so you don't have to worry or feel guilty." This approach to guilt was fostered by modern views of morality that stressed subjective intentional aspects of behavior rather than absolute standards. Emphasis upon the love principle led people to evaluate their behavior in terms of their motives and this was reinforced by a one-sided view of God that stressed "a loving God wouldn't really punish you for this so why should you punish yourself?" Many persons suffering from guilt had trouble accepting this assumption. It sounded appealing but didn't prove helpful.

Other therapists choose to encourage the options of *self-forgiveness, forgiving others*, and *seeking forgiveness from others.* The notions of forgiving self and forgiving the other person are very important, but there is no real assurance of them happening. The offended party may choose not to forgive or even to punish. Persons suffering from guilt may find it impossible to forgive themselves because they feel they have not suffered enough or that they are not sincere enough. In either case, release from guilt is not achieved because a sound base for forgiveness is lacking. The Christian counselor stands in a unique position to present a basis for forgiveness not dependent upon fickle human nature, but upon the authority of God. This possibility can be integrated with other treatment options.

Although four psychological options for dealing with guilt have been discussed separately, they are rarely treated that way in the actual counseling practice. They may be presented to the client in various combinations or sequences. If the counselor understands the biblical basis for forgiveness it may be combined with some of the psychological options. For example, because God has promised to forgive you, you now have a basis for forgiving yourself. The Christian counselor also has the perspective for clearly establishing those differences between God's attitude toward sin and God's love for sinners. This may help people focus on their human potential (option 2), be released from the fear of punishment (option 3), forgive themselves and receive forgiveness from others (option 4), and even be desensitized to sin (option 1). The sinful act isn't as devastating once you realize that God has already provided forgiveness from it. With the work of God through Christ in proper perspective, psychological options may be useful. Without this perspective they lead nowhere except to self-deception and destruction.

Guilt and Other Psychological Disorders

Helping clients deal with guilt is of primary concern to the counselor because guilt is so closely related to other psychological problems. As a young counselor seeing my first clients who were using drugs I was amazed when one of them said to me, "You know what our major problem is, don't you? We can't handle our guilt."

I also discovered that guilt was a major factor in most of the lives of those who came to me suffering from anxiety or depression. A young mother said, "I just begin to get on top of things and I get hit with this awful surge of guilt. It's like I can't function anymore because I remember all the bad things I have done."

Anger and other problems of emotional control are often tied to unresolved guilt. Anger can be a cover-up for guilt and an escape from closeness in relationships. When people would try to get close to Bob he would blow up in their faces. He didn't know why he was doing it and the people he got angry with were certainly confused. His girlfriend Janice said, "I really love this guy. I think he is a wonderful person, but when I try to get close enough to tell him so he just splatters all over the walls and then runs away." After some time in counseling Bob was able to see that the reason he couldn't accept Janice's compliments about him was that he saw himself as anything but nice. He had to deal with this guilt and his feelings of failure before he was ready for a close relationship.

Mood swings are also closely tied to feelings of guilt. In fact, guilt or a person's attempts to deal with guilt may be the causal factor in both sides of the pendulum swing. When Mike feels guilty his mood is down. However, he can only stay there so long and survive. So, he reacts against the guilt by pumping himself up. He decides to be happy, to not have a care in the world. At such times he tells himself there is nothing wrong with him—everything is coming up roses. But the roses only last until the guilt feelings get too strong again. Then down he goes.

42

Many types of *major psychoses* are also tied to guilt. When the guilt has been persistent, without resolution, persons may unknowingly deny aspects of reality in order to survive. They may blame or suspect others in order to find respite from the harsh self-blame. Sometimes, psychologically induced ailments serve to punish them for deeds for which they have not found forgiveness. In her personal story, *Winter Past*, Nancy Smith says of the paralysis she experienced,

I later found that conversion reactions like mine have definite physical symptoms but no identifiable organic source. It is possible for a human being to suffer such great emotional stress that the body can no longer contain the inner conflict and turmoil. The inner emotions seek a physical outlet. This usually has a dramatic onset and the patient, although experiencing genuine symptoms, is not concerned about the consequences of the physical problem. As I look back now, my concern was not that I might never walk again. It was that I knew I had a true emotional problem. Nancy Smith, professing Christian, was going to pieces.[2]

Although some psychoses can be tied to biochemical imbalance it is also clear that in other instances a person's withdrawal from reality may be his or her method of surviving the emotional trauma that has been experienced. When one's system takes all it can take it ceases to function, or moves into the self-protective mode of nonreality.

With the reorganizing of John's company, he was put in a stressful position, a situation he handled well at first, for he was always expecting relief. However, relief never came. As a result, John lost hope and his behavior became strange. Eventually he suffered a nervous breakdown. His wife said, "He felt guilty. He believed the company problems were his fault somehow. I don't even know what he was guilty about." In many cases like John's the need for *emotional shutdown* is prompted by the inability of the person to deal with feelings of guilt which are ever present.

It is clear that whether you are dealing with personal problems, family problems or various types of social ills you will probably be dealing with guilt of some kind. It behooves the counselor, therefore, to find an approach to the problem which will prove sufficient to penetrate the life experience of the counselee.

Guilt Denial

One of the laws of physics is that for every action there is a corresponding reaction. This has proven true in the area of guilt. People sometimes react to feelings of guilt by denial or by refusing to evaluate their behavior by the rules of society. They tell themselves, *I won't be guilty. I'll set my own rules.*

If the decade of the seventies was called the decade of anxiety then the eighties will probably be called the decade of hardness, or lack of conscience. Psychological problems seem to flourish on the extreme poles of guilt. Just as we have seen that an overabundance of unresolved guilt contributes to many psychological problems, minimizing or denying guilt produces disorders of character and social psychopathology. Many psychologists and psychiatrists report that they are seeing more and more persons with character disorders—persons in whom a sense of guilt is often lacking. One doctor said, "I would love to see a simple case of guilty conscience. I'm not even sure they exist anymore."

Just as counselors must wrestle with the difficulty of helping people accept the realities of forgiveness and freedom from guilt, they must also help counselees accept the realities of the hurt and damage their behavior produces for themselves, their families, and society at large. Relativistic ethics and moral standards have been taken to the point where people do not even consider the consequences of their behavior from a right and wrong standpoint. This leads to lack of insight into the needs of others. Bruce said, "I do what feels good to me. I never take the time to think whether or not it feels good to someone else."

Lack of guilt or inadequate conscience is a major problem in people entering into a relationship with God. How do persons decide they need God when they will not consider the possibility of ever having done anything wrong? It is hard to consider the need for a savior when you haven't considered the possibility of sin. Thus, both psychologists and theologians

44

have struggled over the problems of psychopaths and socio-paths who seem not to experience guilt. The challenge is to help people gain a sufficient view of the negative aspects of their behavior so that they can be motivated, first, to come to God, and then to change and become contributors to society and not just destroyers of society. The Bible assigns this task to the Holy Spirit.

> When he comes, he will convict the world of guilt in re-gard to sin and righteousness and judgment.   (John 16:8)

If a person with inadequate conscience comes to Christ it is clearly a miracle. The socialization process has not laid the groundwork by which such a person may see a need for God. Where conscience is inadequate there is no legal guilt, and where there is no guilt a man or woman senses no need for any payment of the penalty for sin. Many modern men and women are saying, in effect, "God is fine for people who need him."

The problem of a lack of guilt or conscience can be even more frustrating from the perspective of non-Christian coun-selors because they have no higher authority to which to point the counselee. They have no one to summon who can demand personal responsibility for behavior. How can such counselors deal with a person when God does not exist and society does not matter? Is it any wonder that our prisons are full and our court dockets are backed up for years? We have no adequate institutional or treatment structure that enables us to retrain people to act in a manner that takes into account the needs of others.

Unfortunately, besides the social problems that are created, "doing one's own thing" or acting without conscience does not meet the needs of the individual either. I have never met a happy sociopath; they are only hardened shells of people going from one exploitation to the next. They define success as not getting caught; but that kind of success has no lasting payoff. Where there are no standards, people rarely feel love, accep-tance, or success. I am describing a problem of crisis propor-tions with which counselors of all types will be heavily involved for many years to come. Only as there is a return to biblical and societal values will attitudes change on a scale large enough to allow us to alleviate the problem.

In the meantime, counselors need to recognize that *traditional verbal counseling has little effect on this type of problem.* You are no match for the con artist. People who do not experience guilt are usually very skilled in manipulating the therapist. Treatment approaches that have been most successful are not based upon *insight,* but upon the ability to *control counselees' behavior and teach new patterns of behavior* which, if not based upon sound views of society, are at least consistent with them.

People gain insight when they are put into a situation where they can clearly see the consequences of their behavior. Unfortunately for persons who suffer from inadequate conscience they usually lose everything that could be near and dear to them before they realize what they are doing. Sometimes conscience develops in prison or in the loneliness of an alley on skid row. Sometimes it never develops at all. Unfortunately we do not know very much about the psychological processes which are involved in such new learning. While we are waiting on such knowledge the counselor must still deal with the backswing of guilt in the best way possible. It is a very frustrating proposition.

Giving Up Guilt

Counselors become painfully aware that some people hold on to their guilt against all odds. They remain guilty when there is no logical reason why they should. Restitution has been made, words of forgiveness have been received, God's forgiveness has been reaffirmed, relationships have been restored, but they are still "guilty." To understand this situation we must ask what function the guilt plays for this person. What is the payoff? What does he or she receive that makes all the pain bearable? If the guilt is to be overcome, its payoff system must be understood and undermined.

One common payoff for guilt is control. After all, people won't expect much when they are bleeding and broken. The feelings of guilt can be turned on and off as needed in order to manipulate those around them. Jennie admitted, "I felt guilt all right, but I used it as a crutch. If I was fearful or didn't want to do something I had a guilt attack. I also learned that when I felt guilty my parents also felt guilty. I could immobilize them any time I wanted to."

Mark's behavior illustrates another aspect of control by guilt. He constantly struggled for attention. He needed to be the center of everything. Unfortunately for him, he and his wife belonged to a small group in which all members were given attention equally. When the others in their group were listening to his wife, he would find an opportunity to interject his bad feelings and thus succeed in having them turn their attention to his remorse. Fortunately, the group leader caught on. He confronted Mark with his behavior and challenged him to invest in others rather than demand attention for himself. It was difficult for Mark, but relinquishing this control by guilt was a major step toward getting his life back in order.

Guilt may also be used by the person who fears success. Most guilt-ridden persons know how to fail but they don't know how to succeed. When opportunity for success arises they become immobilized and rationalize their lack of movement by their negative feelings. "I'm just not worthy." "I could never do that." "I'm so afraid I will hurt somebody again." These phrases are often guilty "smokescreens" to avoid new attempts that might lead to success.

Tom's guilt and fear of success were manifest during vocational counseling. He repeatedly told me what a failure he had been.

"I'm sorry, Tom," I said, "I can't let you wallow in past failures. You have two opportunities here—which are you taking?" Tom was somewhat startled by my directness. He stammered and stuttered trying to find new words of self-protection.

"You have been covering your abilities with remorse over past failures far too long," I continued. "You are going to follow this through if I have to find people to drag you."

Tom finally relented and did follow through. He was successful as I knew he would be. He now had the beginnings of a new structure around which to rebuild his life. I had forced him to forge a success so he would see that he had an alternative to focusing upon his past failure. Turning to failure and guilt no longer had to be automatic.

Gestalt psychologists have identified some other ways in which guilt may be useful for the person. This helps explain why such a person is resistant to change. One of these ways is *introjection*, a process by which persons balance their self-views with the perspective they get from the significant others around them. They try to be what they think others want them to be in order to survive. The process usually begins in early childhood.

A little girl may get a message that she really loves Uncle Mac. This forms the basis for a strong "should." Internally, however, she is afraid of Uncle Mac and actually experiences feelings of dislike and hostility. Guilt over not loving Uncle Mac as she should serves to control her behavior and thus keep her from disrupting the family. Although this may serve a purpose for the moment, keeping peace with parents, it is a very hazardous adaptation. Various degrees of pathology may result as she becomes more and more anxious. In the case of our example, the girl who has always been compliant may override the guilt and become explosively rebellious during adolescence. Parents of such a child are often astounded by the sudden change of behavior. Unfortunately, even though the child has rebelled to escape guilt which she had placed upon herself she is now faced with earned guilt related to her acting out against her parents. If introjection is detected early enough the counselor can help the adolescent and his or her parents work out the conflict; the vicious cycle may be avoided.

Another contribution of Gestalt psychology to our understanding of guilt is called *retroflected resentment*, a process by which resentment is turned to guilt. Through introjection (the process of trying to balance self-views with the views received from others) a child learns to hold onto beliefs that are at odds with his or her internal experience. Society teaches that the child should love, honor, and respect those around him or her. The message to the child is strong and the child complies—but resentment builds. This resentment is changed (retroflected) into feelings of guilt. Thus, guilt serves the purpose of displacing the resentment which could disrupt the relationship with parents or other authority figures. Anger that the person—in this case, the child—might be expressing toward others (the parents) is thus turned on self. If the person were to give up the guilt, the anger would either have no object or would be directed outward and create additional conflict. In other words, what people would like to do to someone else— punish—they do to themselves. An adolescent who feels like killing a parent may thus become suicidal.

Another reaction to retroflected resentment is that people try to do for self what they really wish others would do for them. Frank, age 16, surrounded himself with symbols of softness and warmth. His "nest" was almost feminine at times. What he really wanted was affection and physical closeness from others. Unfortunately, those with whom he sought close relationships withdrew out of fear of his symbols. This made Frank feel even more guilty. He sensed he was unacceptable to friends and he also felt guilt because he was not meeting his parents' demands for masculinity. Without careful under- standing and counseling he might have remained in this trap indefinitely.

Without doubt the psychological issues surrounding guilt are very perplexing. Psychology alone cannot offer the ultimate solution for the problem, which is forgiveness. Neither can psy- chology alone confront the other aspect of the problem— denial of guilt. We see guilt affecting people's lives in so many ways—ways we cannot understand, but ways we dare not deny. Theology alone is also hindered in understanding the dynamics of guilt. They are complex and cannot be explained only in terms of sin and disobedience.

Guilt often serves purposes for the guilty which may have nothing to do with their relationship to God. They feel guilty because they are choosing to focus on those feelings that have a payoff. The choice may be self-defeating, but it is real. In a strange but powerful way, guilt brings psychology and theol- ogy together.[3]

CHAPTER FOUR

THE NEED FOR AN INTEGRATIVE APPROACH TO GUILT

GUILT IS BOTH A THEOLOGICAL AND A PSYCHOLOGICAL ISSUE. Thus, any approach to counseling those who are struggling with unresolved guilt must include both the theological and the psychological perspective. Theologically, in order to understand guilt we must have a clear understanding of the biblical answers to such questions as what is sin?, what are the grounds for expecting forgiveness from sin?, and, even more basic, what is God like? and why can we expect to experience his love?

There are also serious psychological questions to be considered. What roles do anxiety and fear play in regard to guilt? What effect does one's upbringing have upon feelings of guilt?

What are the social reinforcers that may maintain guilt? What is the relationship between earned guilt, which is the result of sin, and unearned guilt, which may be the result of such things as failure to meet someone else's expectations? The stream of questions is both long and deep.

From the armchair it is easy to isolate these and other issues related to guilt and to carefully address the issues one at a time. However, when you are dealing with a real live person who is struggling with guilt the issues may not be as easy to discern. In working with counselees I find myself dealing with theological considerations at times and, at other times, with psychological issues. The majority of the time, however, I find that I must deal with the interaction between the two. By this I mean the counselees' theology may be affected by their psychology, and their psychology may be greatly affected by their theological belief systems. I am constantly asking how does this person's beliefs, feelings, and behavior relate to his or her inability to deal with the problem of guilt. In addressing this type of question certain issues seem essential to sorting out the problem.

UNDERSTANDING WHO GOD IS

Understanding guilt begins with our understanding of God. If we have an inadequate view of God we will not be able to understand sin or forgiveness either. And this leaves us inadequately prepared to deal with guilt.

In asking who is God? we are posing a question that defies our comprehension. God is bigger and greater than our ability to understand. It is instructive, however, to realize that he has chosen to reveal himself to us, and through the Scriptures we can begin to understand a little bit about who he is and how he wants us to relate to him.

Probably thousands of volumes have been written to help us know God better. It would be presumptuous to think that in a few short pages I could add anything to that understanding. I will, however, underscore some of what we do know about God that will help us better counsel those who struggle with guilt. I have chosen to focus on five attributes of God and to state how I feel each of them relates to guilt.

God Is Holy

First, God is holy. In Leviticus 19:2b we read: "Be holy because I, the Lord your God, am holy." This concept is repeated many times in Scripture and it always carries with it the encouragement for us to be like our holy God. He is perfect. He is spotless. He is without sin and he commands us to be like him. Psalm 99 declares God's holiness, ending with the following strong declaration:

> O Lord our God, you answered them; you were to Israel a forgiving God, though you punished their misdeeds. Exalt the Lord our God and worship at his holy mountain, for the Lord our God is holy. (Psalm 99:8, 9)

The theme of God's holiness continues on into the New Testament. It appears in the Gospels (Luke 1:49), in the Epistles (1 Pet. 1:15, 16) and in strong fashion in the book of Revelation. It is difficult to read the following verses without falling on your knees before our great and holy God.

> "Holy, holy, holy
> is the Lord God Almighty,
> who was, and is, and is to come."

> "You are worthy, our Lord and God,
> to receive glory and honor and power,
> for you created all things,
> and by your will they were created
> and have their being." (Rev. 4:8b, 11)

God's holiness demands a response from us. He asks us to be like him. When we are not like him, which is most of the time, the stage is set for real guilt. We feel guilty because we are guilty—guilty of missing the mark, guilty of not being like God.

God Is Just

Closely related to God's holiness is his justice. This characteristic of God is directly tied to the concepts of sin and cleansing and thus directly applicable to the topic of guilt.

If we confess our sins, he is faithful and just and will forgive us our sins and purify us from all unrighteousness.

(1 John 1:9)

God's justice assures us that if we confess our sins we can
receive purification from sin and thus not have to remain in
our guilt. This same theme is introduced by David.

Then I acknowledged my sin to you and did not cover up
my iniquity. I said, "I will confess my transgressions to the
Lord"—and you forgave the guilt of my sin.   (Ps. 32:5)

The characteristic of God we call "just" assures us that he
will deal with us fairly. He is not fickle and he does not play
favorites. He cannot be bribed but on the other hand he will
not fail to do what he has promised to do. Relevant to guilt is
the fact that he has promised to forgive our sin and remember
it no more. The prophet Isaiah put it quite succinctly.

Yet the Lord longs to be gracious to you; he rises to show
you compassion. For the Lord is a God of justice. Blessed
are all who wait for him!   (Isa. 30:18)

God's justice then assures us that we will be treated fairly
and noncapriciously. There will be no surprises, no change of
rules. He will hold us responsible for our sin, but he will also
gladly release us from our sin and guilt if we ask for the forgiveness which Jesus Christ died to provide. The justice of
God would be a frightening thing if it were not for his mercy
shown to us by paying the penalty for sin. This act turned
powerlessness into hope and despair into promise.

You see, at just the right time, when we were still power-
less, Christ died for the ungodly. Very rarely will anyone
die for a righteous man, though for a good man someone
might possibly dare to die. But God demonstrates his love
for us in this: While we were still sinners, Christ died for
us.   (Rom. 5:6–8)

God Is Love

The passage cited above also stresses the third attribute of God, which is his love. God's love is demonstrated in his dying for us and it is further manifest by freeing us from fear and guilt. This truth is carefully discussed in 1 John 4:16–19.

And so we know and rely on the love God has for us. God is love. Whoever lives in love lives in God, and God in him. Love is made complete among us so that we will have confidence on the day of judgment, because in this world we are like him. There is no fear in love. But perfect love drives out fear, because fear has to do with punishment. The man who fears is not made perfect in love. We love because he first loved us.

Although the word *guilt* is not used here it can be implied from the statement that "fear has to do with punishment." The message of this passage is that because of God's love we need not fear punishment for our sin. This is the message of the psalmist which I alluded to earlier.

He does not treat us as our sins deserve or repay us according to our iniquities. For as high as the heavens are above the earth, so great is his love for those who fear him; as far as the east is from the west, so far has he removed our transgressions from us.   (Ps. 103:10–12)

Because God is love and in him is no darkness, he has no desire to see us experience either guilt or punishment for our sin. That was finished when Jesus died. The prophet Ezekiel knew very well what God had in mind. When God was accused of being unjust in punishing Israel for their sins, the prophet in essence said, "Hold it! Think about this."

"Turn away from all your offenses; then sin will not be your downfall. Rid yourselves of all the offenses you have committed, and get a new heart and a new spirit. Why will you die, O house of Israel? For I take no pleasure in the death of anyone," declares the Sovereign Lord. "Repent and live!"   (Ezek. 18:30b–32)

Although we sin and our sin is grievous, it is overwhelmed by God's great love. He does not choose to call us sinners and continually remind us of our sin. He has chosen to buy us back to himself and call us children. Read the following verses and rejoice.

This then is how we know that we belong to the truth, and how we set our hearts at rest in his presence. . . . Dear friends, now we are children of God, and what we will be has not yet been made known. But we know that when he appears, we shall be like him, for we shall see him as he is.
(1 John 3:19, 3)

God Is Merciful

Another characteristic of God that has a bearing upon guilt is his mercy. God does not give us what we deserve; he gives us what he alone is capable of giving, which is mercy. Even in the books of the Bible where law and judgment are stressed the message of mercy is clearly shown.

For the Lord your God is a merciful God; he will not abandon or destroy you or forget the covenant with your forefathers, which he confirmed to them by oath.
(Deut. 4:31)

Without God's mercy there is no hope because our sin and guilt would separate us from him. In Mary's great song of praise to God after she found that she was to give birth to Jesus, she spoke of God's mercy. "His mercy extends to those who fear him, from generation to generation" (Luke 1:50).

Both the apostle Paul and the apostle Peter affirmed the mercy of God as the basis for our hope of being freed from the terrible tragedy of sin.

Paul wrote:

> What then shall we say? Is God unjust? Not at all! For he says to Moses, "I will have mercy on whom I have mercy, and I will have compassion on whom I have compassion." It does not, therefore, depend on man's desire or effort, but on God's mercy. (Rom. 9:14–16)

Peter's proclamation takes the form of worship and praise. He writes:

> Praise be to the God and Father of our Lord Jesus Christ! In his great mercy he has given us new birth into a living hope through the resurrection of Jesus Christ from the dead. (1 Pet. 1:3)

The statement regarding our living hope because of God's great mercy must be applied as a contrast to the feelings accompanying guilt. God does not condemn us to guilt; he calls us to the living hope.

In our counseling we need to patiently introduce people to the better way. Why stay marooned on the island of guilt when there is much more in store for us? People have the ability to choose guilt and suffering and other ways of self-destruction, but through counseling we can teach them to move from where they are to where they need to be. God's attitude is not the problem. It is our attitude that must be altered. "Because of the Lord's great love we are not consumed, for his compassions never fail" (Lam. 3:22).

God Is Forgiving

Finally, we need to look at God's forgiveness. After discussing the frequent and repeated sins of Israel, Nehemiah wrote:

> But you are a forgiving God, gracious and compassionate, slow to anger and abounding in love. Therefore you did not desert them. (Neh. 9:17b)

The prophet Micah emphasized God's forgiveness with a piercing question.

Who is a God like you, who pardons sin and forgives the
transgression of the remnant of his inheritance? You do not
stay angry forever but delight to show mercy.

(Micah 7:18)

The message of God's willingness to forgive permeates all of
Scripture. Undoubtedly it is repeated so often because of the
extent of our sin and guilt. Sin is abundant, but God's power
and willingness to forgive is even more abundant. David wrote
regarding the extent of God's forgiveness, "He forgives *all* my
sins and heals *all* my diseases" (Ps. 103:3).
Daniel stated:

The Lord our God is merciful and forgiving, even though
we have rebelled against him.   (Dan. 9:9)

In the Gospels we have some marvelous accounts of the interactions between Jesus and the people when he offered forgiveness. It is clear that the nature of man is to withhold
forgiveness while the nature of God as demonstrated by Jesus
is to forgive. Notice Jesus' words after being anointed by a sinful woman.

"Therefore, I tell you, her many sins have been forgiven—
for she loved much. But he who has been forgiven loves
little." Then Jesus said to her, "Your sins are forgiven."
The other guests began to say among themselves, "Who is
this who even forgives sins?" Jesus said to the woman,
"Your faith has saved you; go in peace."

(Luke 7:47–50)

Human beings often make the mistake of trying to classify
or judge the extent of sin. We even do this to ourselves by
passing off some of our sins as harmless while stubbornly
clinging to the guilt associated with others. Scripture clearly
points out that no sin is too great for God to clearly forgive.
"But if we walk in the light, as he is in the light, we have
fellowship with one another, and the blood of Jesus, his Son,
purifies us from every sin" (1 John 1:7). (The only exception is

rejection of Christ's death as an atonement for our sin which is sometimes called the unpardonable sin.)

The greater the sin the greater the forgiveness. God does not want us to harbor guilt. Our guilt keeps us from fellowship with him which he greatly desires. Because of this he readily offers forgiveness to all.

As we come to understand God we realize that he is not soft on sin. His holiness and his justice are demanding. Sin, if not dealt with, will separate us from God. It is God's love, mercy, and forgiveness which bring hope to the guilty. As astounding as it seems, God wanted closeness with us so he made it possible. This entire message about who God is must be communicated if we are to deal with guilt. The entire story must be told. It is not enough to frighten people with God's holiness or to try to give them "warm fuzzies" with accounts of his love. God is a total being who shows wrath where there is no repentance, but stands ready and willing to forgive and show mercy when we give our guilty selves to him.

WHAT IS SIN?

It may seem foolish to take time to discuss sin to someone who is already burdened with guilt. I have discovered, however, that guilt is not always based upon an adequate understanding of the biblical perspective of right and wrong. Human beings have a tendency to distort God's picture in order to provide license for sin on the one hand, or to justify their continuing in guilt on the other. There are many aspects of sin but at this point it will suffice to mention two that may need to be understood when counseling persons struggling with guilt.

Sin does not have to be horrible in order to produce guilt. The most common words used in Scripture to describe sin are *chata* (a primary root) in the Old Testament, which means "to miss or go wrong," and *hamartia* in the New Testament, which means "missing the mark."

The other major emphasis regarding sin is disobedience. Guilt-ridden counselees have to deal with the fact that they have deliberately chosen to disobey God. In other words, sin is not just an accident; it is often a choice. I have found it helpful to show people that they choose to sin—but God also chooses

59

to forgive. The extent of the sin is not the issue, but the extent of God's capacity to forgive and his intent to do so are all-important. Even when there is great sin there is great forgiveness. If we overemphasize the heinousness of sin without a corresponding emphasis upon the greatness of God, people become overwhelmed and turn from God because of guilt rather than turning to God that guilt may be removed.

WHAT IS THE BASIS FOR FORGIVENESS?

From a human perspective, forgiveness has a whimsical, unpredictable nature. People seem to forgive if they feel like it. It is anything but automatic. This realization shapes our thinking for we are often influenced in our beliefs about how God works by seeing how humans respond in a similar situation. If your friends or family members have been inconsistent in forgiving you, you will probably be anxious about how God acts. This uncertainty may result in hanging onto guilt or even feeling that forgiveness is dependent upon how you act rather than how God acts.

God is able to consistently and completely forgive our sins because the debt has completely been paid. This truth stands as the very heart of the gospel and thus must be consistently presented as the heart of our Christian faith. Chapter 53 of Isaiah, which is a prophecy of the coming Savior, explains in detail how the death of Jesus Christ the Messiah satisfied God's righteous judgment for sin and brings healing.

> Surely he took up our infirmities and carried our sorrows, yet we considered him stricken by God, smitten by him, and afflicted. But he was pierced for our transgressions, he was crushed for our iniquities; the punishment that brought us peace was upon him, and by his wounds we are healed. We all, like sheep, have gone astray, each of us has turned to his own way; and the Lord has laid on him the iniquity of us all. (Isaiah 53:4–6)

In the New Testament the apostle Paul wrote concerning the death of Christ which makes forgiveness possible.

For he has rescued us from the dominion of darkness and brought us into the kingdom of the Son he loves, in whom we have redemption, the forgiveness of sins.

(Col. 1:13, 14)

From a legal standpoint, then, God forgives on the basis of the debt having been paid. We do not have to continue to feel guilty, because we do not owe God anything. The debt has been paid. In fact, nothing you or I can do adds anything to the forgiveness Christ died to provide. As Jesus said on the cross, "It is finished."

God's righteousness is satisfied. Our freedom from guilt is on layaway. It is all paid for. We only have to pick up the package. This means we must ask for forgiveness and we must believe that God has given it. These two steps go a long way toward freeing a person from guilt and they must be emphasized. When there is forgiveness there need be no guilt. God has gone out of his way to completely secure our forgiveness so that we can become completely free of our guilt. This is the way he wants it. He doesn't want anything between us and him, not even our guilt or remorse over our past.

UNDERSTANDING GUILT PSYCHOLOGICALLY

Just as guilt has a theological side it also is greatly affected by things psychological. When working with an individual it is not always possible to distinguish between guilt and anxiety. Guilt refuses to let loose of the past while anxiety may be fearful of taking hold of the future. On the surface these may appear to be quite the same. Both cause us to feel funny and to act strange. In working with counselees it is important to help them to understand what thoughts may activate their feelings of guilt.

Guilt and Anxiety

Let's begin by examining anxiety. Here are some questions to ask. Are the counselees afraid they will repeat the misdeed? Are they afraid that others will learn of their past? Either situation will lead to feelings of anxiety which can be interpreted as guilt. Until you correct this misinterpretation you cannot deal with the inappropriate feelings of guilt.

Hanging onto guilt may also be a way of trying to avoid thinking about the possibility of repeating the sin. That is to say, guilt may be used as a strong deterrent against the temptations people feel. They choose to emphasize feelings of guilt rather than deal realistically with their feelings about their vulnerability to temptation. This is not usually effective, says Bruce Narramore:

> In fact, guilt feelings do more to frustrate and defeat us than anything else. When we begin to feel guilty and depressed, we soon are of little value to the work of God.[1]

It is much better to help such counselees deal with their vulnerability to temptation rather than have them go on believing that their feelings of guilt over past wrong deeds will be strong enough to deter them from any reoccurrence. Let's be direct. It is safer. The more straightforward we become about the possibility of sin, the greater will be our capacity to evoke God's help and protection. Anxiety and guilt only get between us and God, which means they hinder the application of his grace to our lives.

> No temptation has seized you except what is common to man. And God is faithful; he will not let you be tempted beyond what you can bear. But when you are tempted, he will also provide a way out so that you can stand up under it. (1 Cor. 10:13)

The Psychological Benefits of Guilt

We must also consider that guilt serves a great psychological purpose for many people. Put simply, guilt has a payoff. It serves a purpose.

For many people, the sharing of personal struggles is the only way they feel they can have contact with someone they value. They may come to you as their counselor week after week with the same problem. "I just can't get over feeling guilty," they say. Are they telling you this over and over again because it seems like the only legitimate way to ask for your attention? If the problem of the person is not being affected in

62

any way by your counsel you may wish to ask yourself if you are a solution, or part of the problem. If you are just reinforcing the person's continued wallowing in guilt, you are not serving a useful counseling function. You may want to alter the basis for continued interaction.

I have found it helpful in some instances to say to a counselee, "I am willing to continue to meet with you weekly for a time but I am not willing to discuss your feelings of guilt. I have given you all the help I can for that problem. You know all that I know about it. Now I need to support you as you move on to new aspects of your life."

Guilt and the Past

When you are trying to understand counselees' guilt it is usually helpful to examine the expectations and the treatment they received from their parents. Guilt is a learned response, and in many families the response learned is an inappropriate one. Some persons have never learned to be remorseful regardless of how bad their behavior may be. On the other hand, there are those who have been taught that not only should they feel bad because of their sin, but they should feel bad forever. Such a belief must be attacked before guilt can be adequately treated.

This belief and behavior is obviously inconsistent with Scripture and thus must be attacked both theologically and psychologically. People need to be led to repentance, which is seeing sin as God sees it. However, once they repent and see the sin from God's perspective they are to receive his wonderful forgiveness and immediately go on with life. God neither requires nor desires that they waste time demonstrating how sorry they are. He only wants them to face their sin, confess it and move on without it.

When a person is caught in the trap of trying to deal with sin in the way that parents demand, he or she is usually playing a psychological game that cannot be won because it need not be played in the first place. God is not like ineffective parents. He does not demand that repentance be proven by weeks, months, or years of sorrow. He did not say go and remain preoccupied with your guilt and sorrow. Rather he instructed people to go and sin no more (John 8:11). God desires people's love and adoration, not their wallowing in guilt. Unfortunately this may not be the approach they learned from their parents. If such is the case the counselor has the responsibility of teaching the guilt-ridden person a better way. Instead of reinforcing the preoccupation with sin we need to teach people to magnify God.

EARNED AND UNEARNED GUILT

Have you ever talked to people who said they felt very guilty and yet, as you talked to them, you couldn't really discover any wrongdoing? If so, you may have been dealing with people suffering with unearned guilt. Unearned or pseudo-guilt is a feeling and/or belief that closely approximates the feelings we experience when we have done something wrong. Usually it is not related to what we have done but what we have not done. A clue to watch for is the word *should.* "I should have known better." The words *if only* may also give you a hint. "If only I had studied. . . ." "If only I hadn't gone out that night the house might not have been burned."

Unearned guilt is often tied to rigorous, perfectionist standards. People want to be something they cannot be or to satisfy others' expectations which cannot be satisfied and their dilemma results in thoughts and feelings which cannot be distinguished from guilt. The unmet expectations may come from within or may be passed down by other family members, teachers, pastors or friends. In any case, when the expectations are heard, people feel guilty. They say, *I should have done better. I am really bad.* In some cases it takes the form of mind reading. *I should have known that my wife wanted me to stop for a loaf of bread. Now her dinner will get cold and it is all my fault. If only I weren't so selfish.*

Unearned guilt can be very damaging both in terms of the emotional energy that is wasted and the squelching effect it has on problem solving and problem prevention. Imagine, for example, how much time the man in the example may have wasted feeling guilty about unpurchased bread. He could almost have made homemade dinner rolls in the amount of time he emotionally beat himself. He could have devised a system

64

to assure that he would never forget bread again. Or, he could have enjoyed dinner with his wife and family without bread. In most cases, however, feelings of unearned guilt are expressed and little attention is given to solving the problem, created by an absence of bread or some other issue. Unearned guilt usually prevents us from getting to the ounce of prevention that is worth a pound of cure.

Now contrast unearned guilt with the real thing. Earned guilt is that set of thoughts and feelings that accompany wrong or sinful behavior. In other words, the person with earned guilt feels guilty because he or she *is* guilty. A law has been broken or a person has been hurt. Where there is real guilt the course of action is fairly clear. There needs to be confession, forgiveness, and, in some cases, restitution. Remember that God is ready and willing to take away the guilt of our sins.

Several questions can be asked to help determine whether your counselee is dealing with earned or unearned guilt.

1. Can you say what you have done that is sinful or wrong?
2. If you had to ask forgiveness for some thought or action, what would it be?
3. If you had to ask forgiveness of a person, who would it be?

If the person cannot come up with a clear answer to any of these questions, you are probably dealing with unearned guilt. If you suspect unearned guilt it might be helpful to pursue one or more of the following questions.

1. What expectation do you think you had or have for yourself that you didn't meet?
2. Who are the people you feel you may have let down?
3. Are you putting demands upon yourself which you cannot meet?
4. What action might you take now in order to move yourself closer to where you would like to be emotionally, mentally, or behaviorally?

While earned guilt needs to be handled with confession and the receiving of forgiveness, unearned guilt needs to be met with a well-thought-out plan of action that will help persons come to grips with the expectations driving them to remorse.

In most cases they need to deal with the impossibilities of their perfectionistic thinking.

I sometimes ask, "Could Jesus have satisfied your parents?" This is usually met with a smile of recognition.

In other instances, where people are worried about the effects of their behavior, I ask, "What is the worst thing that could happen?" The worst thing that could happen has probably already happened—they feel guilty and negative about themselves. They have no way to go but up. As a counselor you need to work toward mobilizing people against their fears of further failure. This is usually best done by helping them acknowledge past and present success which they have minimized while dealing with unearned guilt.

PUTTING IT ALL TOGETHER

We began this chapter by stating that guilt must be approached from both a theological and a psychological perspective. Now the question, how do we put the two together?

I believe we begin by examining people's belief systems with them. What do they believe about God? What do they believe about sin? What do they believe about themselves?

Next, we need to try to understand what it is that makes it difficult for persons to accept forgiveness. Are they repeating the unhelpful injunctions they heard from parents during childhood? Are they stopped by anxiety? Are they somehow enjoying or getting a payoff from their feelings of guilt?

When we have answered these and other pertinent questions which may arise then our role may become that of a trainer. We may need to teach them some correct theology which they can use to counteract their errant belief system. If we don't feel comfortable in this role, we should refer them to another counselor or pastor who does. Retraining is very important. Guilt will not be resolved until people have a new, more accurate understanding of their beliefs and the scriptural foundation of those beliefs.

You may also need to do some teaching in the psychological area. For example, you may need to help them understand more fully the impact of their parents upon their life currently. You may need to teach them how to better manage their anxiety so as to cope with fear. Fortunately, there are many helpful books in these areas, written from both Christian and secular perspectives.[2]

Additionally, you may need to stop reinforcing certain behaviors which may only serve to keep them feeling guilty or dependent upon you. Give them attention when they are feeling good, not when they are feeling guilty. Once again, if you don't feel competent in teaching the counselees in the psychological area, refer them to a psychologist or counselor who does. The key to success in counseling is good teaching which leads to good skill development. This is true whether you are talking about intellectual skills such as truth about God and forgiveness, or whether you are talking about psychological skills such as thought control, anxiety management, or how to get unhooked from parental expectations.

To successfully handle problems related to guilt you must keep a broad perspective. If you assume that all problems of guilt are alike, or that each person can be helped according to a predetermined method, you will fail. You must carefully analyze each person's situation separately and then put that person in touch with the type of help he or she needs the most. The God who created us understands even our guilt. It is up to the counselor to put sufferers in touch with the liberating truth about God and also the psychological skills that can set them free.

CHAPTER FIVE

EARNED AND UNEARNED GUILT

IN THE PREVIOUS CHAPTER, reference was made to the need to help counselees distinguish between earned and unearned guilt. Because this distinction is so important this entire chapter will address and illustrate the differences between the two in order that the counselor can in turn help counselees distinguish between them.

When Jeremy first contacted his pastor for counseling he was tearful and depressed. "I just can't do anything right," he said. "I have made a complete mess out of my life."

As they sat and talked, Jeremy's pastor kept expecting to hear a long story of sin and degradation. He had heard it before. He knew how easy it is for guys to mess up their lives. With Jeremy, however, it seemed different. He hadn't

69

stepped out on his wife, nor was he using drugs or embezzling funds. As far as the pastor could tell he wasn't even a chronic liar. Jeremy's devotional life seemed to be intact and he wasn't neglecting his family. Finally the pastor said, "Jeremy, I know you are torn up with guilt, but I can't do anything for you until you help me understand you better. I'm not sure what it is that you have done. Do you know the reason for your guilt?"

Jeremy stuttered and stammered for a time, but he couldn't put his finger on anything. "I just feel wrong about everything I do," he said. "In fact, I also feel terrible about the things I don't do. I have reached a place where I find it hard to look my wife and children in the face."

Although the pastor was cautious he realized that he was not dealing with the typical sin-and-need-for-repentance type of problem. He recognized that the young man's guilt was unearned. Jeremy's feelings of remorse were identical to those experienced by persons who were clearly sinning, but the objective reasons for the feelings were absent. His guilt was real, the feelings were there, but they were unearned.

CLASSIFICATIONS OF GUILT

It is important to realize that you cannot distinguish between earned and unearned guilt on the basis of counselees' feelings. The feelings act as vital signs that tell you and the person that something is wrong. They do not tell you *what* is wrong. Careful listening and sensitive probing is necessary to ferret out the conditions behind the feelings.

I have found it helpful to look for two types of earned guilt and two types of unearned guilt. These four categories cover most of the guilt situations I have encountered in counseling.

True Guilt

I define earned guilt as true guilt. The persons feel guilty because they have done or are doing something wrong. They feel guilty because they are responsible. They have violated God's standards or the law. They have missed the mark.

As was discussed in chapter 2, the conviction of the Holy Spirit may produce true guilt, an awareness of the legal responsibility for our behavior and feelings of remorse. Ezra's prayer shows the impact of true guilt upon a person's life.

O my God, I am too ashamed and disgraced to lift up my face to you, my God, because our sins are higher than our heads and our guilt has reached to the heavens. From the days of our forefathers until now, our guilt has been great. Because of our sins, we and our kings and our priests have been subjected to the sword and captivity, to pillage and humiliation at the hand of foreign kings, as it is today.

(Ezra 9:6, 7)

True guilt is resolved by confession, restoration where possible, and acceptance of the forgiveness extended by God and the offended person.

The first type of true guilt is *active.* It deals with ongoing sinful behavior that is unresolved. The person needs to cease and desist; as Jesus said, he or she is to "go and sin no more." Although the sin may occur again, the person needs to confess it and to receive God's forgiveness. This transaction can be complete and is not dependent upon the person's ability to forsake the sin. Receiving forgiveness should not be confused with receiving the power to forsake the sin.

Inability to forsake the sin often leads to the second type of true guilt, which I call *unfinished.* Unfinished true guilt has been forgiven but it is still a part of the person's life because of the struggle. Intellectually people know that God forgives seventy times seven, but when they struggle against repeating the sin they often do not feel forgiven.

A female counselee said, "For a person who has been washed clean I sure feel dirty at times. Even when I am tempted and am victorious I get dragged right back into the guilt of the old situation." At this point the guilt is unfinished because she can't draw a boundary between the past and the struggle of the present.

Another feature of true, unfinished guilt can be seen in those situations where the sin may have been confessed and forgiveness received but all the consequences of the sin have not been experienced. Jack said, "I knew my church had forgiven me for

71

the money I took and I knew God had forgiven me, but the reminders just kept coming up." Each time he would see a church member on the street he would be flooded with guilt. On occasions he would turn away, hoping he had not been recognized. He found himself confessing his sin over and over. The pressure mounted and Jack became more and more disturbed. Finally in desperation he mounted his courage and went back to his pastor. The pastor listened carefully and then said, "Jack, you have prayed for forgiveness long enough. God is not deaf. He has heard and answered each and every one of your prayers. It is time to finish this thing. Each time that you are reminded of your sin, instead of feeling guilty and asking for forgiveness, I want you to praise God for the forgiveness you have already received. You have prayed for forgiveness and it has been received. Now you are to praise God for that forgiveness."

Jack followed the pastor's suggestions and his guilt soon began to dissipate. Turning from prayer to praise had brought closure to the matter and he was finally free from his guilt.

Unearned Guilt

Like true, earned guilt, unearned guilt also takes on different dimensions. One type of unearned guilt revolves around shame over past behavior. The shame is not related to a specific sin but more to a pattern of life. The person feels incapable of doing the good thing, often feeling inadequate or incompetent. Reflecting on this type of guilt, psychologist Karen Horney writes,

> . . . a neurotic person is often inclined to account for his sufferings by feeling that he does not deserve any better. This feeling may be quite vague and indefinite, or it may be attached to thoughts or activities which are socially tabooed, such as masturbation, incest wishes, death wishes toward relatives. Such a person usually tends to feel guilty at the slightest occasion. If someone asks to see him his first reaction is to expect recrimination for something he has done. If friends do not come or write for some time he asks himself whether he has offended them. If anything goes wrong he assumes that it was his fault. Even if others

72

are blatantly in the wrong, have definitely mistreated him, he still manages to blame himself for it. If there is any collision of interests or any argument he is inclined to assume blindly that the others are right.[1]

Cheryl's life was often shrouded by shame and unearned guilt. She attacked her own person and surrounded herself with shoulds. "If I just had more character . . ." she would say. "I should be able to handle things better. I just never do the right thing." Because of these feelings, Cheryl developed a pattern of behavior that affected her whole lifestyle. She was constantly under a cloud. Even though she was well liked and greatly talented, her shame kept her from putting her life together.

Shame is a subjective state—which may or may not indicate the appropriateness of unearned guilt. Unearned guilt may involve shame or it may not. It depends upon the psychological makeup of the person involved.

Dr. Andrew Lester has provided a helpful diagram that shows the different origins of guilt and shame. Shame comes from our view of our ideal self while guilt comes from the conscience. Both threaten the person's view of self.[2]

We feel shame when we are not living up to what we feel we should be (ideal self) whether we are sinning or not. We feel guilt when we are going against our moral principles or our conscience. This may involve sin or unearned guilt due to not meeting others' standards.

When people suffer from shame they often fight against changing that emotional state even when they are objectively aware that they need not be where they are. Cheryl's counselor brought her to a place where she could say, "I don't have anything to be ashamed of." On a day-by-day basis, however, she had to learn to stop focusing on her shame and to act on her awareness of the good things God wanted to do in her life.

Some people who suffer from shame do such a good job in communicating it to others that they are avoided. This increases their false guilt and the downward spiral is intensified. They feel like people are avoiding them and indeed they are right.

I believe a major ministry of the body of Christ is to learn how effectively to help such persons. Instead of allowing them to continually focus upon their feelings of shame, which only increases such feelings, we need to call them to be all they can be and then support them spiritually and emotionally as they leave their shame and seek to realize their full potential. Unearned guilt expressed as shame is a crippler. It needs to be challenged.

Failure to Meet Expectations

A second type of unearned guilt results from failure to meet expectations. As I explored with Ben his deep feelings of remorse I became aware that I hadn't heard him describe anything he had done which might warrant his feeling so guilty. We were going around in circles; he wasn't getting any help and I was becoming more and more frustrated.

Finally I said, "Ben, which one of the commandments have you broken?" He thought for a while and then said, "Well, none I hope."

"Have you broken any laws?" I asked.

"Not on purpose," he replied.

"Okay then," I continued, "who is it that you really feel you have let down?"

Ben became solemn and tearful at this point and finally said,

"I'm sure I have never pleased my parents. They expect so much of me and I just can't do it. I really let them down."

"Now we are getting somewhere," I replied. "Your problem isn't guilt—it is disappointment over unmet expectations."

The more Ben and I talked about his inability to please his parents the more he realized how fearful he had become. "Sometimes I can't even move," he said.

Inability to meet others' expectations leads to fear, which leads to the incapacity to meet other expectations which are more simple. Once again, a vicious cycle has been created which, without intervention, will cripple the person. When such a cycle has begun, another emotion invariably is involved—anger.

"Ben," I said, "if people were putting this type of demand on me I would get pretty angry." At first he denied it and took more blame on himself.

"They don't really ask much," he said. "I'm just not whom they want me to be." As we talked, however, it became more and more apparent that his false guilt was now serving as a check on the intense anger he was feeling. He was afraid to own the anger for fear of not being able to control himself.

Finally I said, "Ben, you don't have to hurt anybody but you do have to be honest with yourself. Your parents have been very unfair with you at times and you are not helping yourself or them by denying it." Slowly but surely the anger was expressed and I was able to teach Ben some new ways of dealing with himself and his parents. Once he was able to set his own realistic standards he was on the way to freedom from the unearned guilt that had crippled him.

Some people's unearned guilt is related to not being able to meet their own standards. "I should have been able to please him," Julie said of her estranged husband. "I wanted so badly to be a good wife and I failed." The facts of the case did not warrant Julie's verdict. She had been a good wife even though that had not prevented her husband from following through on some of the lustful thoughts which had plagued him from youth.

"The problem was not your inadequacy," I said. "The problem was Brian's sin. He had this weakness in the sexual area long before he met you." Sobbing silently, Julie said, "I guess down deep I knew that, but I so wanted things to be different. I thought if I was the right kind of wife I could help him through the problem." I reminded Julie that as much as we would like to, we can't change anyone but ourselves.

The process of healing for Julie involved a realization that even though Brian had not changed and even though he had done some things, including leaving her, which had hurt her deeply, she had done what she had set out to do. She had met her goal.

"I loved him sometimes when he wasn't very lovely," she realized. "I guess I did do what I tried to do but it sure didn't work out." Julie needed to grieve the loss of Brian and the failure of the marriage, but she did not need to cover her grief with the unearned guilt of unmet personal expectations.

The Unmet Expectations of a Peer Group

Another source of unearned guilt may be the expectations of the peer group or other important group such as the church. When my wife was a new Christian she was told by her church family that she should not wear lipstick. She met this expectation for a while but then she came to believe that to wear or not wear lipstick has little or nothing to do with her relationship with God. When she made the decision to return in moderation to her makeup she became aware that some people felt let down by her decision. Some even implied that if she wasn't careful she would slip from the faith. If it were not for the strong support she received from a respected Christian couple she might have fallen prey to false guilt because she was not meeting the expectations of her church family. Fortunately, she was able to work through this without the negative effects false guilt produces.

Adolescents often struggle with unearned guilt stemming from peer group expectations or conflicts between the expectations of their peer group and parents or conflicting peer groups such as church and school. Some adolescents have enough ego strength to stand against one or both of the peer groups. Others cannot stand against either and may even feel the pressure of guilt from both directions. Counselors need to remain alert to these pressures and help their counselees recognize and verbalize these conflicting situations.

Donna said, "If I please my parents I can't please my peers. I'm so confused I don't know what is right."

Allen struggled between the expectations of his Fellowship of Christian Athletes group and his pals on the basketball team. He felt guilty because he really wanted to be accepted by both. His counselor pressed him.

"Allen, you are going to feel guilty until you decide for *you*. You can't please everyone and you will feel this unearned guilt until you decide what is right for you."

MAKING YOUR COUNSELING EFFORTS COUNT

Effective counseling requires both avoiding counterproductive behavior and the application of productive efforts. If the problems of earned and unearned guilt are to be addressed, counselors need to make their efforts count. We will first look at the negative actions that need to be avoided.

Avoiding Negative Responses

Counseling time and effort are often wasted when the counselor fails to properly understand the nature of the problem posed by the counselee. If the true guilt of the counselee is minimized and treated as unearned guilt he or she will not be helped by discussions of shame or failure to meet expectations. Earned guilt is only relieved by guiding the person to forgiveness. On the other hand, if forgiveness is emphasized when there is no real offense the counselee will be denied the opportunity to work through the problem. The counselor needs to exercise prayerful discernment before pressing the counselee to a course of action related to the guilt expressed.

In addition to carefully listening, the counselor needs to exercise caution in prescribing feelings for the counselee. It is not very helpful to tell a person, "I really don't see any reason for you to feel that way." The fact is the person does feel that way and telling him or her otherwise will only create a new source of unearned guilt. The problem is a problem of perception, and problems in perception are not solved by logic. Self-discovery is called for. Questions are much more effective than declarative statements.

"Ray," his counselor asked, "when you feel this way, whom do you feel you have sinned against?"

"I'm not sure," Ray replied. "Maybe it isn't so much that I feel I have sinned, I just haven't done what I wanted to." At this point Ray is still open to learn. If he had been told what he should feel he would have been closed to further exploration. I have counseled dozens of clients who have struggled for many extra years with their guilt because they have been told what to feel instead of being helped to work through the feelings they have.

Other negative responses the counselor or pastor should avoid are providing pat answers or imposing solutions. These two are combined because they both involve telling the counselee what to do and they both result in lack of action on the part of the counselee.

Stan was told that he had to have faith that God would forgive him. What the counselor didn't realize was that Stan had tried and tried to exercise faith, but had only become more and more confused when his feelings of guilt remained. The counselor's words were true but not very helpful. Stan didn't need a pat answer. He needed someone to help him understand faith and forgiveness and to stand behind him as he learned what faith was all about. I have found it productive to help the counselee translate the pat answer into specific behavior.

"Stan," I asked, "if you trust God to forgive you how do you feel you will act and how will you feel?"

"Well, I suppose I could feel happy and I could act happy," he answered. "I could also thank God for his forgiveness." Faith is most effective when it is translated into behavior. Pat answers are not useful unless the counselee knows how to put them into practice.

Imposing solutions upon the counselee is also a problem because the solution may not be integrated into the feelings and thoughts of the counselee. Forcing a person to apologize and ask for forgiveness may not be helpful if the counselee is struggling with unearned guilt. Even in cases of earned guilt the counselee may be forced to act before he or she understands or is committed to the action. This will only result in confusion and eventually lead to new guilt when the person realizes that he or she has not been authentic.

The keys to avoiding errors posed by pat answers and imposed solutions are time and patience. The counselor may hurry to solve the problem but the solution is not the counselor's but the counselee's. Counselees must find solutions to their guilt which they can understand and put into operation. Going through the motions is not enough—the effective counselor recognizes that the solution is in the eyes or experience of the counselee.

One other common error needs to be addressed. That is taking responsibility away from the counselee. You cannot find forgiveness or freedom from expectations for the counselees. They must do it for themselves.

Matt was really struggling with unearned guilt which resulted from his not being able to meet his father's expectations. His counselor helped him understand the problem and then said, "We need to confront your dad about this." Matt was afraid but could not voice his fears to his counselor any better than he could his father. The result was that the counselor talked to the father for Matt. He aired some of Matt's frustrations without the father changing or Matt learning any new skills. Taking this responsibility did not help. Matt's guilt was intensified because he not only felt bad about not helping the counselor confront his father; he also felt guilty because he took responsibility for the conflict which resulted between the counselor and the father. The story might have been different if the counselor had prepared Matt to confront his father for himself and then supported him as he did so.

Taking responsibility for clients does not equip them and it does not give them the help they need to get free from their guilt, either earned or unearned.

Implementing Positive Responses

Because guilt is so closely tied to the emotions of a counselee the first task of the counselor is to help the counselee clarify his or her feelings. This action will help the counselor and the

79

counselee to distinguish between earned and unearned guilt and will also help the counselor to understand the counselee. When counselees feel understood they are more likely to continue in their efforts to deal with their guilt.

Guilt is often accompanied by impacted feelings, that is, a confusion of feelings or the presence of intense feelings of which the counselee is not consciously aware. Impacted feelings are like a tangled ball of yarn. It requires patience and careful attention to find the ends and eventually untangle the snarls. If you make the mistake of grabbing a string and pulling on it before you understand the problem you will only tighten the snarl. Listening to help clarify the feelings is much like tenderly turning the ball of yarn until the solution to the entanglement is found.

In helping counselees with impacted feelings care must be taken to help them discover their feelings for themselves. Premature interpretation may result in more confusion on the counselee's part and thus slow down the process of dealing with the source of guilt.

A second positive response to problems of guilt is to help counselees discover their own resources.

Michelle's pastor was aware that as she struggled with her guilt she was setting aside many of the spiritual resources she had. Finally he asked a series of questions that got to the real issues.

"Michelle, what do you know about God that can help you with your guilt?"

At first she said she didn't understand.

"What does God say about your sins?" he continued.

"I guess they are forgiven."

"You *guess?*" the pastor asked with a smile.

"I know God forgives," she said as she smiled back. At that point God was once again a resource for Michelle. She had been led to look beyond her guilt to the possibilities.

Michelle's pastor also recognized that guilt-ridden people often try to make it alone. He challenged her position by asking, "Who are the people you can really count on to encourage you through this tough time?" She hadn't thought about the role that friends and family often play in healing. As she was able to draw close to them she found comfort and strength.

Persons struggling with guilt often fear failing again. They can be helped by realizing their resources in dealing with temptation and by being put in touch with the joys of worship. Praising God is a great way of getting beyond guilt.

A third constructive response to problems of guilt, earned or unearned, is to teach the counselee new skills. Reference was made earlier to teaching people how to have faith. Some people don't know how to accept forgiveness. They may have never received forgiveness from their parents so someone needs to show them what it is all about. Many people have a mental conception of faith and forgiveness and joy, but they have never learned how to experience or live them out.

In cases of unearned guilt counselees may need to learn how to confront effectively or how to be assertive. Counselors can assist them by sharing what they themselves have found helpful, or what they have seen help others. Some counselees are helped by learning how to tell themselves the truth or by learning to stop their obsessional thoughts. Others may need to learn how to apply the truths of Scripture to specific situations related to their guilt. Never assume that people have the intellectual or emotional skills they need to deal with their guilt. Be ready to walk them through each situation and to provide them with new alternatives as they struggle with their guilt. We are to teach and we are to encourage. The writer of Hebrews said it well:

Let us hold unswervingly to the hope we profess, for he who promised is faithful. And let us consider how we may spur one another on toward love and good deeds. Let us not give up meeting together, as some are in the habit of doing, but let us encourage one another—and all the more as you see the Day approaching. (Heb. 10:23–25)

The counselor's work is not finished until counselees are functioning beyond their guilt, or, stated another way, until guilt no longer has a hold on them. As the counselor sees clients take the steps to deal constructively with their problems he or she needs to reinforce and encourage those steps of growth and maturity. Sometimes the steps are gradual and may be almost indiscernible by the counselee. The effective counselor can retrace those steps of progress for the counselees so that they can be encouraged to go on to further progress. One person said, "I think the thing my counselor did which was most helpful was to believe in me until I could believe in myself."

Often when counselees do not have a sense of direction the counselor can show them the progress they are making. One counselee said, "It was neat. My friend helped me to realize that I was on the right track. I didn't have much confidence, but when he stood behind me I knew I didn't have to just sit around and feel sorry for myself." As he continued to work on his feelings of remorse he was cheered along the way. He really identified with Hebrews 12:12, "Therefore, strengthen your feeble arms and weak knees."

Whether the guilt is earned or unearned the process is the same. It is Jesus Christ and his family who bring healing.

CHAPTER SIX

THE PROBLEM OF MOTIVATION
BY GUILT

WHEN COUNSELING PERSONS SUFFERING WITH GUILT it is important to realize that a part of their problem is how they were raised. A major training tactic used in our culture is for parents to attempt to motivate by guilt. Consider these phrases:

"Your mother and I will be very unhappy with you."

"If you were a true Christian you wouldn't even consider such a thing."

"Don't let me down."

"You are a real disappointment to your mother."

Those subjected to this type of indoctrination will have trouble with guilt even if they live impeccable lives. They have become so sensitized to what others, including God, might think that they respond with feelings of shame to almost everything they think or do.

Margaret said, "In my head I know that the things I am doing are not wrong, but I still hear my mother saying, 'If you really care about us you will do better.' I feel so guilty I second-guess everything I do."

Motivation by guilt is an attempt to produce action or behavior change by implicitly or explicitly indicating that if persons do not act or change they should be ashamed or feel guilty. It is often summed up in some form of the phrase, "shame on you." Augsburger writes:

> Our first feelings of guilt do come from others. They are born in a child's mind when his parents scold him. They spring from the fear that a parent's love may turn to hostility.
>
> All through our maturing years, our fear of the taboos of our family and friends gives birth to guilt feelings. These vary, of course, according to the moral and social standards that are found in our society.[1]

WHY NOT MOTIVATE BY GUILT?

There are several good reasons for not using the motivation-by-guilt approach. If we as counselors can convey these ideas to parents, teachers, and others, we will prevent some of the problems related to guilt and thus spare people much grief.

Jesus did not rely on the motivation-by-guilt method. If we are to be like him then we need to emulate as many of his patterns of interaction with people as possible. It is exciting to note that when Jesus was talking to Peter about his denial he did not use guilt as a means of motivation. Jesus avoided every opportunity to rub Peter's nose in his sin. Instead, Jesus dealt with Peter by the use of questions and strong positive statements. "Do you love me? . . . Tend my sheep . . . shepherd my sheep . . . shepherd my sheep." Peter had repented and had suffered for his sin. The motivational message from Jesus was "I have work for you to do." The Lord didn't find it necessary to say, "You know, Peter, because you have been a bad person and because you sinned against me, you had better do my work." There was no threat and no attempt to shame, just the statement of opportunity.

Other statements by Jesus are also noteworthy because of their lack of motivation by guilt. "Go and sin no more." "Pick up your bed and walk." "Follow me." All of these provide direction without the disadvantage of creating unneeded emotional stress. Jesus truly understood people and their psychological needs.

A second reason for not motivating by guilt is that it doesn't work anyway. When people are constantly barraged by guilt-producing statements they become deaf to the motivational aspects and remember only the guilt aspects. There is no evidence that guilt-ridden children are more obedient or more efficient children. More likely, the opposite is true. They get so wrapped up in their feelings of shame and remorse that they fail to follow through on the requests made of them.

People become deaf to motivation by guilt in the same way that they became deaf to the boy who cried wolf. Guilty people are not more responsive; they are just more guilty. Unfortunately we attempt to correct their lack of responsiveness by creating more guilt. No wonder our counseling offices are full!

Motivation by guilt should also be avoided because it results in side effects that are incompatible with healthy personality growth. Paul Tournier has written:

Social suggestion is then the source of innumerable feelings of guilt. A disapproving silence, a scornful or mocking look, a remark, often thoughtlessly made, may well amount to a powerful suggestion. Thus, a girl is weeping on the day after her father's death. 'Don't cry for your father,' her mother flings at her; 'he died because you were not a good girl; now you will obey me!'

The last phrase provides a clue to the feelings that drive the mother, in her confusion, to say such things to her daughter: anguish at finding herself alone to bring up the child, and anxiety to make sure, from the start, that she will be obedient. But she does not calculate how ineradicable such a suggestion may be. Even without any such assertions by the parents, we often find that the idea

grows in a child's mind that he is guilty of the death of a
father, a brother or a sister, and that the death is a punishment for his own disobedience.[2]

Feelings of inferiority, low self-esteem, lying to cover up
mistakes, aggressive behavior, bragging, withdrawal, and self-
punishment are some of the side effects of motivation by guilt
which I have observed. These side effects contribute to an
increase of both earned and unearned guilt as discussed in
chapter 5. They will only be avoided as we begin to have an
influence upon the ways people, especially parents, seek to
motivate. We need to teach and preach a more positive approach, and if we don't we will never succeed in guiding people to the place Scripture encourages us to be. There is no
substitute for teaching people to view themselves and their sin
from God's perspective. This includes being positive in the
many places where Scripture is positive.

A final reason for not motivating by guilt is that better alternatives are available. Even if motivation by guilt worked without the negative side effects it would still not be the best
method by which to train people.

SUBSTITUTES FOR MOTIVATION BY GUILT

Scripture emphasizes several methods which when used together are a wonderful substitute for motivation by guilt.

The first is *encouragement*. Notice Hebrews 3:13:

But encourage one another daily, as long as it is called
Today, so that none of you may be hardened by sin's de-
ceitfulness.

To encourage is to help people know what they are doing
right, not just what they have done wrong. It involves walking
with, not talking *at*. In Hebrews 10:24 we are told that we are
to meet together regularly in order to stimulate one another to
love and good deeds. The method given for doing this is encouragement. Encouragement involves praise, support, and a
spirit of togetherness. In contrast, motivation by guilt usually
involves criticism, isolation, and blame.

Scripture also points to the need for *exhortation* as a means of motivation. Exhortation and motivation by guilt are not the same thing. Exhortation deals with facts. To exhort is to lay the truth on the line. Exhortation emphasizes the truth and the natural consequences of not following the truth. In contrast, motivation by guilt focuses upon the person and the negative aspects of the person. It is often a matter of attitude. I find it difficult to fit motivation by guilt into the attitude Paul admonishes us to have.

> Brothers, if someone is caught in a sin, you who are spiritual should restore him gently. But watch yourself, or you also may be tempted. (Gal. 6:1)

The most effective exhorters are those who gently but strongly lead the way. They don't want people to feel guilty because people who feel guilty usually lag behind.

Ephesians 4 emphasizes another alternative to motivation by guilt. We are instructed to *equip*. People need to be shown and they need to be taught how to do things. This is what equipping is. It is not just telling people that they should feel guilty because of what they haven't done. The most effective parents and teachers are those who show their children what to do and how to do it.

Derek said with a smile, "My dad taught me how." Edward, on the other hand, said, "My dad told me I was stupid and that I never do anything right." One of these young men may need to spend hours in the counseling office. The other could become the counselor. You can guess which will be which.

Whether it is enabling people to serve God or just to live in a complex world equipping involves showing, telling, and leading people until they have enough experience to carry on themselves. Jesus spent three years equipping his disciples. I'm sure they would have enjoyed three more!

In considering alternatives to motivation by guilt counselors need to realize that they are often in a position of needing to retrain those who feel guilty because they have been previously trained by guilt. Some counselors use the same method in retraining and compound the damage.

Confronting the Problems of Those Motivated by Guilt

Counselees who have been motivated by guilt usually treat themselves in the same way. They try to get over feeling guilty by making themselves feel guilty about feeling guilty. "I shouldn't be feeling this way. If I were a better person I wouldn't be this way." Bruce Narramore comments:

Let's say people come up to you and say, "You're a lousy, miserable sinner." They berate you, threaten to reject you, and in general let you know they think you're a mess. In other words, they make you feel immensely guilty. Your natural reaction to this guilt might be to give up and agree with their negative evaluation. You may think to yourself, *They're right. I really am a mess.* By agreeing with their evaluation, you participate in their condemnation of yourself.[3]

The counselor's job is to show the person a better way. I have found that this is best done by gently directing the person to try some new things. For example, I said, "Ken, what do you think would happen if instead of telling yourself, 'I'm so stupid' you would say, 'This may be hard but I'll do as much as I can. It doesn't have to be perfect'?"

Ken's response was noncommittal. "I don't know but I guess I could try." Laughingly I pointed out, "You just had your first success. You said you could try and you didn't run yourself down. We are going to keep at this until you develop some brand new habits."

Each time Ken spoke more hopefully or optimistically during the counseling sessions I would point out that he was making headway. Each time he spoke about himself or his behavior in a derogatory manner I would stop him, smile, and say, "Would you like to try that again without the guilt trip?" It was difficult at first and he had to be stopped numerous times, but it wasn't long until the pattern began to change.

After Ken had learned to detect guilt-tied statements during the counseling session, I had him begin to stop himself when he would use them during the other parts of his week. When he began to do this the old habit was broken. He was on the way to a new type of freedom. Motivation by guilt produces bondage whether the statements come from self or others. Freedom comes only when the source of motivation by guilt is confronted.

Several considerations must be kept in mind as you confront persons who have been motivated by guilt. First, their responses may be so automatic that they are not even aware of how they have been programmed to feel guilty. They need to be able to *take a look at themselves* and see the way they are treating themselves. They may be out from under their parents or poor teachers but they still live with the injunctions from the past. If they can describe what is going on now they can then be directed to look for new ways of viewing themselves.

I asked Kyle why he carried his parents around in his pocket. He seemed confused at first. I said, "They live in your shirt pocket and they have a little transmitter which sends messages loudly enough to be heard only by you. Guess what the messages say?" He sat silently.

"Let me turn up the volume," I said. "Tell me when you can hear it." Starting softly and then increasing the volume dramatically I said, "Guilty, guilty, *guilty,* GUILTY!" He got the message and was then ready for the relearning process to begin.

After self-awareness is enhanced people need to be guided to *look for a better way.* "Betty," I said, "how would you have liked to have been treated by your mother? What kind of things would you have liked to have heard from her?" At first Betty couldn't come up with any answers. I could see the guilt begin to rise. I responded with a series of inquiries.

"Do you think you would have liked to be told you were doing a good job? How about 'you speak very clearly,' or 'you have a clear voice'?"

"I would have liked both of those," she said. I smiled and she knew she was getting the picture.

People who have been motivated by guilt have difficulty determining what they want. They have not learned that it is okay to want to be treated decently. They have put their normal thoughts and feelings aside and seem to meditate only upon their badness. Normal responses need to be gently drawn out of them. After Betty became aware of how she would have liked to have been treated by her mother I had her go through the process of considering how she would like to treat herself. Both were essential to the healing process.

As people discover new ways to treat themselves they need to *practice* them. Betty had to be taught to say the kind of things to herself that she wished her mother would have said to her. When she would fail to do so her immediate response was to feel guilty.

"You're feeling guilty because you're down on yourself," I said.

"Yeah, I am," she replied.

"What else could you tell yourself?" I queried.

"Well," she said, "I suppose I could say, 'Give yourself a break, you're not as negative as you were last week!'" This process was repeated over and over again during counseling and she was taught to do it for herself outside the counseling session.

Practice doesn't make perfect but it is essential. Persons who have been trained by guilt have practiced under this method for years. As new methods are acquired it will take months or years of practice before the new ways become permanent.

The counselor needs to be prepared to *help people deal with the emotions* they feel as they begin to stop clubbing themselves with guilt. Guilt-ridden people don't usually allow themselves to feel anger. However, as they begin to improve they may suddenly become overwhelmed by what they are feeling inside. Anger often becomes a predominant concern as the person is freed to think and feel something other than guilt.

Lloyd said, "I don't understand it but all of a sudden I am feeling really ripped off by my parents. I'm mad at them for all the garbage they piled upon me." I pointed out to Lloyd that being able to acknowledge his feelings without feeling guilty was a first step in being released from that past. This paved the way for him to be able to forgive his parents and thus escape the new guilt that an unforgiving spirit might have brought. Careful guidance was necessary to help him feel the anger without slipping into revenge, which is sin, and which will produce more guilt.

I had Lloyd read Ephesians 4:26 and tell me how it could relate to his feelings toward his parents.

> In your anger do not sin: Do not let the sun go down while you are still angry.

Together we concluded that his anger would become sin if he tried to get back at his parents. Once this choice was made it became easier for him to forgive and go on with his life.

Fear is another common emotional response of those who are dealing with the results of being motivated by guilt. Gary said, "When I realized I didn't have to feel guilty all the time I was really frightened because I didn't know how to feel. Even though I didn't like the old feelings I was used to them. I had to start all over and that was scary."

The counselor can teach people that fear is normal and that they don't have to feel guilty when they experience it. When dealing with guilt-ridden adults it may be helpful to remind them that their guilt has frozen them in time. They have aged chronologically, but emotionally they have been stopped at a younger age as though frozen. If, for example, they had been "frozen" at age eight it would be normal for them to fear what an eight-year-old might fear. If emotionally frozen at age 15 they will fear what a fifteen-year-old fears. Once the emotions are recognized and are dealt with, new growth may take place rapidly.

Rick, age 27, said, "Well, I just turned sixteen today."

"What does a sixteen-year-old fear?" I asked. "We need to know what we are dealing with here."

"All the things I've been fearing," he replied. He didn't need to feel guilty about feeling fear or fearful about his guilt. He laughed and I knew he was on his way.

Self-punishment is another common response in the lives of people who have been motivated by guilt. If you feel guilty you may deceive yourself into believing that you will feel better if you punish yourself. This view creates more guilt, which results in more self-punishment. The counselor's role is to help the counselee break the cycle. In some cases this may involve the use of good theological teaching about forgiveness. In other cases it may involve heavily structured retraining of patterns of thinking, feeling, and doing. In any case it cannot be ignored. Motivation by guilt has taken its toll and must be challenged.

Tony felt guilty because he had not consistently had victory over the problem of masturbation. He knew all the right answers about forgiveness. He even believed that God's grace extends to reoccurring sin. When he had originally sought counseling he said, "I guess my problem is that I can't stand prosperity. Every time something good happens to me I ruin it all. I got a promotion and I got drunk and didn't show up the next day. I have a beautiful wife and family but I spend more time feeling sorry for myself than I do with them." It took several sessions, but the counselor was finally able to help Tony see his life differently. He was helped to see the promotion and the nice family as special gifts from God which God gave to him to enjoy whether or not the undesired habit was under total control. Tony was also helped to realize that piling further guilt and punishment upon himself was not in God's plan.

"Christ received the punishment for your sin on the cross, Tony," the wise counselor said. "It was to help you to live in that realization so you can praise God rather than punish yourself."

By using this approach the counselor was able to direct Tony back to God and away from the destructive feelings that were robbing him of the freedom from guilt that God intended.

We have looked specifically at motivation by guilt because of the tremendous impact it has upon the developing individual. Problems of guilt are particularly resistant to change when people have been trained to feel guilty. The counselor is well advised to carefully analyze this area in the life of counselees in order to determine the type of help and or training which might be indicated. Narramore and Counts write:

As adults, when we fall short of our ideals, our punitive-self goes into action. It evokes threats of punishment, rejection or loss of self-esteem, the feelings we experience as guilt. Only as we gain insight into how these punitive pressures work can we make lasting progress in overcoming their negative influence and turning our energies to more positive life pursuits.[4]

Motivation by guilt creates a network which is self-perpetuating. Parents affect each other; they in turn are affected by their own parents. Both of these parts of the larger family affect the children or grandchildren. Even though the counselor may not be able to deal with the entire family structure it is important to help the individual see how his or her feelings of guilt may have been affected by the system. The counselee must at least unhook from the motivation-by-guilt system mentally, even if physical separation isn't possible. This process requires a good deal of support from the counselor and the family-like resource, the church. We must make every effort to create the type of structure that will help address problems of motivation by guilt rather than perpetuating them. We must help break these chains of guilt.

CHAPTER SEVEN

LOVE AND GUILT

WHEN NATHAN FINALLY SOUGHT COUNSELING he was at the
end of his string. His self-hatred had reached the point where
he had planned to take his life. A discerning friend knew something was going on and finally persuaded Nathan to confide in
him. The friend listened as Nathan poured out his inner feelings. The more Nathan talked the more it became apparent
that he could not forgive himself for hurting so deeply those he
loved.

"I'm so ashamed," he said. "They loved so much and all I did
was hurt them."

The friend said, "Nathan, I read somewhere in the Bible that
love can cover a multitude of sins. I wonder if that applies to
your situation? You said your parents love you so much and I

have heard you talk about God's love. I wonder if there is some hope?"

After talking about the verse (1 Peter 4:8) together, Nathan and his friend decided there were three ways that love could cover Nathan's sin: God's love for him, love from his parents and friends, and Nathan's love and forgiveness toward himself. God's love is the enabler that allows Nathan to express the last two loves.

> In *The Four Loves*, C. S. Lewis makes this insightful statement: The [natural] loves prove that they are unworthy to take the place of God by the fact that they cannot even remain themselves and do what they promise to do without God's help.[1]

GUILT AND GOD'S LOVE

There is a tendency among those who suffer from unresolved guilt to have a high view of their sin and a low view of God. Where the condition exists there is a need for getting the person to take a much closer look at who God is and how he loves.

> This is how God showed his love among us: He sent his one and only Son into the world that we might live through him. This is love: not that we loved God, but that he loved us and sent his Son as an atoning sacrifice for our sins. (1 John 4:9, 10)

It is clear that God's love has covered (atoned for) our sins. I have found it helpful to say to counselees, "You may still feel bad about your sin but you need to know that God is not stuck on it. He has more important things to think about. Christ died so that sins could be forgiven and right living restored." Emphasize the right living, not the sin.

Fear of God's judgment is sometimes a factor in guilt because people have been trained to fear rather than to accept forgiveness. When God's judgment is strongly stressed in an attempt to deter sin there is often a carry-over of guilt even after the person has sought God's forgiveness. I have found the writings of John to be helpful at this point.

There is no fear in love. But perfect love drives out fear, because fear has to do with punishment. The man who fears is not made perfect in love.   (1 John 4:18)

The last sentence, "The man who fears is not made perfect in love," can be applied in at least two ways. It may refer to a person who has not received Christ and therefore has reason to fear. He is still under judgment. It may also apply to the believer in whom God's love is not perfected or fully realized. God's love is not complete until it is incorporated by persons in their consideration of life on a day-by-day basis. The intent of his love is that people be totally free from the penalty and the shame of their sin. I like to view God's love as the hiding place from our sin. We are hidden from sin so that it has no more claim on us. In the case of Nathan cited above, he had to learn this great truth before he could begin to believe that life was worth living.

I have been greatly moved by the fact that when persons are capable of understanding and receiving God's great love they spend less and less time talking about their concerns with guilt. David talked to Nathan the prophet and to God about his sin, but he talked to the multitudes about God's love. In fact, when David was able to fully receive God's love he was through dealing with his sin. Anything less than a repentance and a full return to God's love leaves the person handicapped and guilt-ridden.

GUILT AND HUMAN LOVE

The love of parents and friends holds tremendous possibilities for the person who suffers from guilt. John Powell points to the type of human love which is most needed and what it costs to want to give it.

A meaningful life can result only from the experience of love, and this implies a commitment and dedication to another. Love rejects the question "What am I getting out of this?" as the only criterion of fulfillment. Love understands by direct experience those often-quoted words of Francis of Assisi: "It is in giving that we receive."[2]

97

To withhold love because of sin is to leave the guilty person in bondage even if God's love has been received. People have trouble clinging to their awareness of forgiveness from a God they cannot see when they are not being loved and forgiven by people they do see.

Tearfully, Anita related the story of taking her parents' bankcard and using it to get money from the automatic teller. She told of getting caught by her mother, begging for forgiveness, and promising never to do it again. She had confessed her sin in the only way she knew how and had demonstrated her repentance with five years of not stealing a penny. What broke her heart now was the fact that after all that time her mother still referred to Anita as a thief. Her mother held the incident over her head as though it had just happened. And when friends said to Anita that it wasn't her fault or that her mom was wrong, it helped very little. These facts could not take away Anita's deep feelings of failure and rejection. She needed the love of her mother extending forgiveness and acceptance to put the stealing incident clearly into the past where it belonged.

Restoration of loving relationships after sin is often the mark of victory. We know that forgiveness has been received because love is present. "[Love] . . . keeps no record of wrongs" (1 Cor. 13:5b).

Human love is also a key factor in dealing with issues of unearned guilt. As was stated earlier, unearned guilt may result from not meeting the expectations of friends or family. Subtle or not-so-subtle pressure from parents may result in feelings of guilt. To communicate disappointment toward some people is to shatter their confidence and cause them to feel shame. Often when this happens, these people will not be restored until the parent or friend is able to recognize what has happened and frees them from the expectations. For example, after a time of miscommunication, my wife said to our daughter, "I'm sorry I criticized you. I *do not* expect you to be perfect." Unfortunately, parents often react defensively. They may refuse to consider the possibility that they are creating pressure for their children. In such cases the relationship is harmed and feelings of unearned guilt remain.

As a sophomore, my son Mike was working hard to make the varsity wrestling team at his school. The competition was fierce and some days he wondered if he could handle it. I tried to encourage him and would often say things like, "I think you can beat Tracy" or "I think you can beat Brian." Unfortunately, what Mike heard was not the encouragement but the pressure. He heard me say, "If you don't beat Tracy and Brian, I will be disappointed." He became more and more tense and when he would have a bad day he would feel guilty. He had little awareness of how proud I was that he was even in the competition. As this continued, he got more and more down on himself and our relationship began to suffer; he withdrew from me and when he was near me he was often angry. One day I realized what was happening and after checking out my perceptions with my wife I approached Mike.

"Son," I said, "when I tell you that you can beat Tracy, what do you hear?"

"I don't know," he said, "I guess I feel like a failure. I feel you won't be happy if I don't beat him."

At that point I asked Mike to forgive me for that kind of pressure and assured him that I was looking forward to watching him wrestle even if he could never beat Tracy. He thanked me and I could tell that some of the pressure was released. We were able to talk about it and at times when I would "backslide" and begin to push too hard he was able to ask me to back off. Our love was growing and it was beginning to create freedom from the unearned guilt of parental expectations.

The love of friends and family can also have a curative effect. It is helpful for people to talk through their feelings. Sometimes we need to hear ourselves express our feelings before we can really see the distortions that may be there.

June said, "When my mom lets me talk and doesn't try to tell me how I should feel I usually realize where I am confused and then I feel better." The most loving thing to do for friends or family members who suffer from either earned or unearned guilt is to ask them questions that will help them understand themselves and their feelings. The least productive and, therefore, the least loving approach is to tell them how they "should" feel.

Stuart said, "I don't need to be told that my feelings are stupid. I already know there is something wrong. What I need is to figure out where I am mixed up. My friends are better help than my parents because they listen more and don't talk as much."

Love can make a difference in matters of guilt—especially the patient kind of love that says, "I have time for you. I have time to be with you as you sort out your life." Love says, "Tell me more. I value you as a person and I want to help you to value yourself more."

Paul Welter writes:

The "natural" helper, then, is one who is effective in his own life, is motivated by love, and is willing to work hard enough that helping skills become automatic. And he reaches out, not down, to help someone. (This method was demonstrated very clearly by the life of Jesus. He didn't reach down to help, he *came* down, and reached out.) Perhaps the most important way the "natural" helper helps is that he serves as a model for his friend.[3]

GUILT AND SELF-LOVE

Although the term *self-love* is often controversial, most would agree that people need to treat themselves with the same degree of love and respect which God shows to them. God loves me and he forgives me, therefore I need to love me and forgive me. I am not perfect, but I have value. In fact, I have too much value to God and to others to waste my life by choosing to keep myself under the condemnation of past actions which God has already wiped off my account. To love myself is to refuse to keep charging myself with crimes that have already been forgiven. If I am no longer being charged with a crime by God, what purpose does it serve for me to continue to condemn myself?

Self-love is not a narcissistic or self-centered goal. It is a central part of seeing ourselves as God sees us. We should learn to value ourselves, both because God values us and because we will then be able to love God and others more. This, then, is the first step in learning to love ourselves. We must make a commitment to seeing ourselves as God sees us. We must acknowledge to ourselves, *God, You have made me in Your image and made me to live eternally with You. Like Adam and Eve and all other members of the human race, I have sinned and marred that image. But Christ has paid the penalty for my sins. I know that You want me to recognize these facts. I know that You want me to lovingly respect myself and every other member of the human race.* [4]

Some people fear self-love because they feel it will lead to pride or slothfulness. I have found, however, that when I am loving myself I not only forgive myself for past sins but I encourage myself to go forward to new and better levels of living. Forgiveness by God and forgiveness of self can lead to higher standards and more acceptable behavior. It is a mistake to believe that if you forgive yourself you will be more apt to do other bad things. Instead, we need to realize that it is a matter of choice. When I sin and receive forgiveness from God and myself I am still faced with a choice the next time temptation comes. I can choose to hurt myself by sinning again or I can choose to love myself by doing the good. Counselees need to be helped to realize that self-hatred does not lead to the right choice. In fact, it is love of self that may open the door to the better choice.

When self-love leads to right choices then love does cover a multitude of sins. Andy said, "I finally came to the place of realizing that I loved myself too much to continue to punish myself and I love myself too much to continue hurting myself by choosing to sin. I don't choose the best thing all the time but I'm working on it. For the first time in my life I feel like I want to do something better than self-destruct."

GUILT AND LOVING DIFFICULTIES

Counselors often deal with persons whose difficulty in handling guilt is related to specific problems of giving and receiving love. One such problem area is the difficulty of receiving love unconditionally when they have only experienced conditional love.

Duane expressed it well. "I don't trust this forgiveness stuff. There has to be a hook. I have never been loved without people wanting or expecting something out of me." Lucy expressed similar feelings: "My parents loved me all right, but I always had the feeling that it was hanging by a thin thread. Somehow I felt that if I stepped out of line even a little bit they would take back all the forgiveness they had offered in the past."

The counselor's role in this type of situation is to patiently help the counselee come to understand that God's ways are not man's ways. His love is a higher love. In fact, he loves us too much to include the hook. I have helped counselees by using the "what if—as if" approach.

"What if" God really is able to love in this way? How do you think you would feel? How do you think you would view your past? How would you act differently? What kind of choices would you make? Normally, the answers are very freeing. The counselees realize that they have greatly restricted themselves because of their fear that his love has conditions which they can't meet. Intellectually they may be able to say the right things about God's love, but emotionally they don't feel it.

The "as if" part of the solution is sometimes more difficult. I ask my counselees to go an entire day living as if God's love and forgiveness were unconditional. In other words, I ask them to live out for a whole day the answers to the questions "what if."

Lucy said it was really strange at first. "I'm glad you didn't ask me to do it more than a day. I would constantly catch myself acting as though God's love were conditioned. Then I would have to stop myself and get my mind where I wanted it."

After hearing Lucy's story and applauding her success, I asked her if she was ready to build on what she had learned by practicing for longer periods of time. She had some failure days but after a time the success outweighed the failures. It was a great day in her life when she was able to say, "I'm not just acting 'as if' anymore. I really do feel loved."

Sometimes living the truth is necessary to shape our ability to believe and feel the truth. Counselors need to work hard to help counselees who have known only conditional love come to realize the freeing potential of God's unconditional love and forgiveness.

NEEDED: NEW BRIDGES

Another difficulty in applying the truth about God's love to guilt is what I call the absence of bridges. If you think of human life as past, present, and future you can recognize the need for continuity. If a person has not felt loved or forgiven in the past he or she will surely have difficulty in the present and will fear the future because of the inability to expect the good.

When people have misperceived the past they may also misperceive the present and the future. In these situations bridges must be built which will provide the basis for freedom from guilt from each time period.

Nancy had grown up under very nonforgiving conditions. Her parents made her pay for her sins even though they would sometimes talk about God forgiving them. As Nancy became an adult she could remember almost everything she had ever done and she felt guilty for it. She went to a counselor who helped her receive healing for those memories, enabling her to see Jesus as forgiving her and accepting her. "I went from total fear," Nancy said, "to seeing myself as one of the children talked about in Matthew:

Jesus said, "Let the little children come to me, and do not hinder them, for the kingdom of heaven belongs to such as these." (Matt. 19:14)

Although Nancy's experience of dealing with the past was helpful to her she had trouble applying that same love of God to her adolescence and early adulthood. Her experience of God's love needed to be bridged from one life stage to the next. For most people this happens automatically but for Nancy it had been missing and she needed to catch up on God's love, so to speak, before the guilt could be left behind.

Nancy's counselor asked her to talk about the negative experiences that were prominent in her memory and helped her focus upon the truth of God's forgiveness in each experience. Because Nancy is a visual person the counselor helped her by telling her to close her eyes and picture Jesus extending his arms of forgiveness. She was asked to do this for each situation. Bridges were being built and fears which cause unearned guilt were being weakened. The counselor then took Nancy into the future.

Instead of imagining God's wrath, which was a part of Nancy's fear, the counselor asked her to imagine Jesus being her advocate. "Jesus is the greatest defense attorney in the world," the counselor said. "He makes Perry Mason sound like an amateur. Can you see him declaring you as free from guilt? He is saying 'This is one of my children. Her guilt has been charged to my account and paid.'"

In dealing with guilt it is essential to build these bridges because people have a natural tendency to compartmentalize their lives and not see the relationship between past forgiveness and future possibilities. Until these bridges are established, persons will continue to suffer from the guilt of the past and the present and will experience unearned guilt as they face an uncertain future.

Finally, people have difficulty receiving love and forgiveness when they have been conditioned by harshness. Gary's parents yelled at him a lot and even though he knew down deep that his dad was forgiving, he would still feel guilty every time his dad raised his voice. Gary said, "I even feel guilty when he yells at my sister. When his voice raises, so do my negative feelings. It's hard to feel loved or forgiven when inside you are all torn apart."

Gary's counselor helped Gary distinguish between guilt over what he had done and unearned guilt that would be stirred up by his father's harshness. Once Gary was able to separate the two in his mind he was able to begin to deal with them correctly. He learned to tell himself that just because Dad raised his voice he didn't have to start punishing himself, when he hadn't even done anything.

People who have been abused as children often have a particularly difficult time accepting love. Somehow they feel they don't deserve it. If counseling is to be effective with such people they must be led into a new awareness of God's love and the love of others around them. Until this happens they will struggle.

Yes, love does cover a multitude of sins, but it often takes patience and hours of careful listening to help the counselee receive what they need most. Love frees from guilt.

CHAPTER EIGHT

RELATIONSHIPS AND GUILT

You will not counsel very long before you encounter persons who do not have a clear-cut notion of who they are. These people usually have destructive levels of dependency on others and cannot envision their worth apart from these other people. They seem to live and breathe for the approval of those who are important in their lives. This approval is often provided or withheld in a capricious manner, leaving these people constantly wondering about their own value. The "important others" are usually the type of people psychologically who seek to use the dependent person to meet their own needs. They could be called incomplete persons for they seek to use their children or others dependent upon them to complete them. They are needy persons who convince those caught in relationships with them that they themselves have deep needs that cannot be met outside of their "special" relationship. This is what we call an *enmeshed relationship*. The term *symbiotic* is also used to describe this type of relationship. It means "to live together" or "mutual dependence."

> We may have all the trappings of adulthood and live much of our lives as responsible, competent people, free to make our own decisions and create our own lives. But with our parents, we may feel at the mercy of old patterns of response that, though deeply unsatisfying, frustrating, and draining of our energies, seem beyond our ability to change. We are not free and can't be free when we're still more concerned with taking care of our parents' feelings than our own and when we are still caught up in trying to win their love or avoid their displeasure.[1]

When lives are enmeshed, issues of individual responsibility become very clouded. Therefore, issues of guilt are confused and need to be clarified through counseling. The enmeshed person usually feels both angry and guilty, but also believes that nothing can be done about it.

TYPES OF ENMESHED RELATIONSHIPS

In my experience, 25 to 30 percent of those who seek counseling are involved in some type of enmeshed relationship. These relationships may involve parents, siblings, friends, pastors, teachers, other authority figures, and religious gurus.

We will discuss several examples of enmeshed relationships and show how the issues of guilt may become confused in each. Guilt may be assumed because of implications passed on by the important other person or it may be denied as a defense against being seen as a bad person. It is common for persons from all types of enmeshed relationships to interpret anxiety or feelings of inadequacy as guilt. The examples below will highlight some of the important issues.

Inappropriate Parent-Child Relationships

Chuck said, "I can't leave my parents. They need me too much. I can't live without them. Our relationship is very special."

Chuck is forty-one years old and has always lived with his parents. He tried moving away on several occasions but always came back. On one return he reported that his mother said, "I knew you would be back. Our relationship is too important for you to waste it by moving away." His father said, "I hope you have gotten that foolishness out of your head. Your mother needs you."

Dr. Dorthea McArthur calls persons such as Chuck "impinged-upon adults." She has identified several commandments these persons have received from their parents which keep them in these unhealthy relationships. Remember, these persons have been stopped in the normal progress of life. They have been deprived of the right to grow.

Here are some of the commandments outlined by Dr. McArthur[2] which I believe have a very big part in creating problems of guilt for the enmeshed adult who is "impinged upon." They may not be stated in the following words, but they are communicated repeatedly nevertheless.

1. You will not be a whole, separate person, but remain a perfect part of me (usually given by mother).

2. We will need and cling to your failures as an affirmation of our dependence upon each other (usually given by mother).

3. You will see badness in yourself and see it in others who take you away from me. You may not express any negative feelings, especially anger, about our relationship (usually given by mother).

4. You will obey your mother's wishes without question or anger. I will support her in any form of discipline or sabotage she chooses to use. . . . I will not consider your feelings (usually given by father).

5. If you disobey these commandments, I will disapprove and will tell our friends that you are ungrateful, unloving, and uncaring. If you obey, I will ignore you with my continual

absence. I can never love you as a whole person (usually given by father).

These commandments may sound far-fetched to those who have grown up in a healthy home, but for the person who has been indoctrinated by these or similar communications, the problems with guilt are very real. Several problems seem to come up often.

Seeing Oneself as Incomplete

Jill recognized the *problem of not seeing herself as separate from her mother* (Commandment One, mother). She said, "My mother doesn't have to try to make me feel guilty—I'm that way all the time." As Jill and I discussed the things she felt most guilty about it was clear that she was not an evil or sinful person. Her thoughts and actions for which she felt guilty were not wrong. In fact, most of her thinking was wholesome and her actions very defensible. After weeks of working through her entangled thoughts and feelings we concluded that her guilt was not related to sin but to her desire to be an independent person. Even though Jill was married she had not given herself permission to leave her parents emotionally. It was helpful for her to realize that leaving parents is not only a good idea. It is a directive from God.

> Therefore shall a man leave his father and his mother, and shall cleave unto his wife; and they shall be one flesh.
> (Gen. 2:24 KJV)

Focusing on Failures

Patty's life is an example of *having a relationship with parents which is focused upon failures.* A very competent person, Patty was a potential teenage suicide. She had tried once and failed and was leaning toward trying again when we first talked. "I can never please them," she said. "I hear over and over and over again about the dumb mistakes I made as a child but never about anything good that happened. There must have been something positive that I did or said that they could remember."

Patty could not think about being with her parents without being flooded with feelings of guilt. "Friday night," she said, "the family all eats together and it is 'Let's review how bad you kids were.' It must make their (the parents) whole week."

Lives and relationships that focus upon failure will produce guilt, depression, and anger. Patty had certainly been provoked to wrath (see Ephesians 6:4). Unfortunately, she was assuming guilt that was not hers and was taking out the anger and wrath upon herself. She was obeying the first half of Number 3, seeing badness in herself—but she was not able to fulfill the last part of the commandment, You may not express any negative feelings.

This illustrates a third problem with guilt from enmeshed relationships. *People come to see all feelings as evil.*

Unfortunately, the more Patty tried to suppress her angry feelings the more guilt she experienced, and the more she wanted to do away with herself. She was caught in a vicious circle. As she saw badness in herself she also at least subconsciously saw the injustice and felt angry. This resulted in intensified feelings of badness and then anger. Thus her view was that she must inflict upon herself the ultimate punishment—suicide.

Such dilemmas are not solved by simple injunction. Even telling her that her thinking was distorted increased her feelings of worthlessness. I needed to lovingly let her express her anger and help her to see that the anger in and of itself was not wrong. I reinforced the fact that she had chosen not to take revenge against her mother, and I encouraged her to let me help her search for solutions that did not demand that she take revenge against herself. The struggle was a long one, but she made it. In the process she learned that feelings are not automatically evil, but are sometimes helpful in that they force us to see where the problem areas in our life may be. She was angry because she was being coerced into believing a lie—the lie that said she was bad and should constantly feel guilty.

Another problem with guilt stemming from improper parent-child relationships is that of *believing that the beliefs, wishes, or desires of others should never be questioned.* Dick's father insisted that he do everything his mother asked. This was difficult because she was very inconsistent and inconsiderate of Dick's circumstances and his own needs.

"She is uncanny," he said. "Every time I have something planned for me she seems to know it, and then forces me to do something that she wants. One time it was so dumb," he said angrily. "She made me stay home to watch the dog. We had never had to watch the dog before and we have never had to since. It was a way to keep me home."

The feelings of disappointment which Dick felt were never acknowledged. In fact, the implication was that he should have guessed that the dog needed to be watched and that he should feel guilty for not having volunteered. The issue of whether or not the mother's request was reasonable was never open for question. When parents are always right and children—even when grown—are never right, the result is very predictable: unearned guilt.

Disobedience

Another problem with guilt which stems from enmeshed parent-child relationships can be seen in Number 5, above. *Disobedience* is not seen just as disobedience but is guilt-compounded by the parents' adding labels such as unloving, ungrateful, and uncaring. These labels are usually not true but are taken at face value by the son or daughter who has been trained to believe and assent to whatever the parents say.

Here are some examples of the way this commandment may be given which I have heard from counselees. "That was the most unthoughtful thing that anyone has ever done to me. If you love me even a little bit how could you have disobeyed me? Doesn't it mean anything to you that your mother and I have sacrificed so much for you? What kind of a person are you? Don't you care at all?" And finally, the most dreaded: "Thanks for nothing! I'm not sure you should even bother to come home if that is the kind of person you are."

In each of these remarks the message is clear; the person is to consider himself or herself totally rotten and should beg for the mercy of the parent. The problem, however, is that these parents only use the begging as a means of tying the person more tightly to them with strong ropes of guilt. If the son or daughter, whom I would call a victim, is not helped to see this and to break the ropes, he or she will be chronically overcome with guilt. Anytime the rightness or wrongness of one's behavior is left totally to the judgment of the parent the problems with guilt will be severe and long lasting.

Scripture is clear. Each of us has a responsibility to examine his or her own life and behavior before God and then either to confess sins and receive forgiveness, or to see what was not wrong or sinful, and therefore rejoice. I have found that helping counselees understand the following verses has been most helpful.

My dear children, I write this to you so that you will not sin. But if anybody does sin, we have one who speaks to the Father in our defense—Jesus Christ, the Righteous One. He is the atoning sacrifice for our sins, and not only for ours but also for the sins of the whole world.
(1 John 2:1, 2)

Each one should test his own actions. Then he can take pride in himself, without comparing himself to somebody else, for each one should carry his own load. (Gal. 6:4, 5)

As you work with counselees who are struggling with guilt, examine their backgrounds very sensitively but carefully. You will probably find some commandments or injunctions which they have received from parents which are keeping them trapped in their feelings of guilt. These parental teachings have been accepted as truth. They are just as true for the counselees as if they had been spoken by God himself. Knowing this, you will need to move slowly in challenging them because your challenges may be seen as an attack on the parents. In fact, the counselees may have been warned by the parents that someone might try to come between them, the parents and your counselees, by telling them bad things about the parents.

I use indirect techniques and rely on counselees' belief in God and in Scripture, and their subconscious doubts, to break through the resistance. Here are some questions I have found useful.

"Do you know any Scripture that would be in conflict with

what your parents have implied?" If they say no, I might say, "I know a couple of passages that may apply. Are you interested in studying them?" If they say no I will postpone it until they are more open.

Another useful question is, "What do you think is true and what may be false about what your parents said?" This diffuses the idea that you are calling their parents liars or are suggesting that they should see the parents as bad.

I sometimes ask, "Your parents see you this way. How do you think God sees you?" The response is usually, "I don't know." Then I can read some applicable Scripture as an answer to my own question.

Finally, I use the hypothetical approach.

"Let's suppose for a minute that these things your parents have been saying and implying were not true. If this were the case, why do you feel they would be doing such a thing?" This allows me to introduce the concept of incompleteness as a replacement for the labeling of the parents as hateful, evil, or even demonic. The counselee usually won't have an answer for the hypothetical question. This gives the counselor the opportunity to suggest a variety of possibilities, such as: "They may need to keep you dependent upon them." "They may not know a better way." "They may actually believe that they are helping you by keeping you dependent upon them." "They may be incomplete themselves without keeping you as a part of them rather than as an independent person."

I often draw the pictures below to point out the problems in the relationship.

Many a client identifies readily with this visual aid and then can be helped to learn how his or her guilt could become so great when they see themselves as an extension of the parents rather than separate people. It is a wonderful privilege to help persons who have felt guilty for years because of inappropriate parent-child relationships be released to begin living lives of their own—lives which then have the potential for becoming less encumbered by guilt.

GUILT-PRODUCING FRIENDSHIPS

It is not uncommon for persons to be involved in friendships that become a major source of guilt. Usually this occurs in those situations where the friends are not accepting each other as equals and are not taking equal responsibility for the friendship. Gary Inrig writes concerning the dangers in friendship,

> There are two danger areas in friendship. One is that we will choose the wrong friends. Because of peer pressure or our own needs, we associate with the kind of people who can only hurt us. . . . But even if we avoid choosing the wrong friends, we can fall into a second problem, that of forming the wrong friendships. If a friendship is not solidly based, it either will not last or it will drag us down. Over and over, I have seen friendships between Christians harm both people because that friendship was grounded in the wrong things.[3]

Friendships produce guilt when they are grounded in one person's fighting for acceptance by trying to meet the needs of the other. Charles said, "I want to be a good friend but no matter how much I do for Earl I just can't please him."

I responded, "Charles, what if it isn't your problem? What if Earl doesn't have the capacity to offer you the acceptance you need? What if you did everything perfectly in the relationship and Earl couldn't respond? Is it possible that you are feeling ineffective and guilty over something that is outside your control?" Such questions were sobering for Charles, but were essential to his finding relief from his nagging guilt.

Barbara's friendship with Sue produced guilt because Barbara was too dependent. She believed she could not survive without Sue. Sue would handle the pressure for a while and then she would retreat. This left Barbara feeling that she had done something wrong and that she was a bad person. Both feelings resulted in severe guilt. As Barbara was able to control her neediness the friendship became healthier and the guilt began to lessen.

Friendships that produce guilt do drag us down. People need to be encouraged to set realistic expectations for friendships and for their own behavior in the friendship. People who enter into relationships expecting that the friendship will meet all their needs usually come away defeated and feeling guilty. Their needs create an intensity in the relationship that is very destructive. Friends are to be enjoyed, not smothered. In a like manner, friendships are to be contributed to, not just taken from. When people are too dependent upon their friends they often become selfish and, in the process, feel unloved. Once again Inrig's insights are very helpful.

> Some people have difficulty developing friendships just because they are so intense about their friends that they literally smother friendship. They see every moment of weakness on the part of a friend—bad humor or moodiness—as a sign that the friendship is in trouble. They are very sensitive to imagined slights and are easily offended. As a result, they always seem to be watching their friends, and one can never relax and enjoy being a friend. Friendship involves a confidence in the other person that is very giving, but also undemanding. Friendship is to be enjoyed, not endlessly analyzed. . . .[4]

In considering guilt-producing friendships we must keep in mind that some friendships are inappropriate and may produce sin and guilt because they are the wrong kinds of friendships. In such cases the guilt is earned guilt and can be resolved by severing the relationship. Abusive relationships and inappropriate sexual relationships are two examples.

In our contemporary Christian culture it is becoming more and more common for single men or women to become friends with married persons of the opposite sex. These relationships often begin innocently enough but may become more romantic than platonic. It is easy to see that they may lead to inappropriate behavior between the two people and, of course, guilt. I do not believe that opposite-sex friendships are bad or sinful. In fact, in another place I have written in their defense. I do, however, believe that they must be approached very carefully and sexual contact must be avoided. Usually the joys of friendship turn to guilt once the two people focus on the physical. When married people have opposite-sex friends, care must be taken that the spouse is comfortable with the friendship. A person should not try to maintain an active friendship with someone to whom they have been romantically drawn.

> I believe male-female relationships which focus on friendships and caring are invaluable to our growth as persons. They help us find our meaning along the broader spectrum of human experience. When they become exploitive, they have ceased to be valid friendships. Caution, not fear, should accompany our care for the opposite sex. Should we refuse to trust God here, we will miss an important area of relationships.[5]

Abusive relationships, whether verbal or physical, usually produce guilt both for the abuser and the one abused. Abusers usually experience earned guilt as the result of their behavior, while the victim may experience guilt as the result of being dehumanized.

The first step in counseling in such situations is to prevent the abuse. It is unwise to devote time to any counseling efforts while circumstances are such that it continues; as the abuse goes on, the guilt mounts. Once the abuse is stopped the counselor can help counselees work through issues of responsibility and forgiveness that will deal with the real guilt and also begin to impact any unearned guilt present.

In recent years much attention has been drawn to the problem of sexual abuse and incest in the Christian community. The problems are very real and can no longer be denied. When incest takes place in a home all members of the family are severely affected. Both the offender and the victim feel guilty, the other parent feels guilty for not knowing and stopping it, and even the nonabused children feel guilty. I have discussed the effects incest has upon the family in *A Silence to Be Broken.*[6] It will suffice at this point to say that after the abuse is stopped each family member must be helped to deal with the guilt he or she is experiencing. Usually this is best done by combining professional help with pastoral care and loving support from the church family. Please note that the guilt cannot be dealt with unless the legal aspects of the problem are considered. Sexual abuse is a crime and must be treated as such. Counselors in such cases must interact not only with the people involved but also with the law and the social service system.

Generally speaking, friendships may produce guilt when they encourage dependency and/or when they become coercive. Guilt is reduced when people take responsibility for their own behavior and are able to say no to those who encourage them to act contrary to what they feel is right. I often ask people who are plagued with guilt, "Who is making your decisions for you?" Decisions are the control tower of life. When the wrong person is pushing the buttons errors will occur and guilt will result.

"Kyle," I said, "if you make a bad decision you can correct it or live with the consequences. When you let others make the decisions for you, you feel guilty for not being in control—but you will also feel guilty for trying to correct the situation."

God places a high priority on individual responsibility and choice.

But if serving the Lord seems undesirable to you, then choose for yourselves this day whom you will serve, whether the gods your forefathers served beyond the River, or the gods of the Amorites, in whose land you are living. But as for me and my household, we will serve the Lord.   (Josh. 24:15)

When people are coerced into things they wouldn't normally choose, or are allowed to cop out on their responsibilities to make good choices, the result will be guilt. I encouraged Kyle to spend less time lamenting his past failures to choose and to spend more time learning to make the kinds of choices that will help him feel competent and responsible in the best sense of the word.

GUILT FROM THE GURU

Wherever there are strong religious leaders people are waiting in line to follow. People are often like sheep being led to the slaughter. The truth of Scripture is often distorted and replaced by the power of personality with the result usually that men and women give up their personal power and become slaves to a system of "truth." Gurus stress loyalty and emphasize the need for strict obedience. When followers get out of line or dare to think their own thoughts they feel guilty.

This same kind of dynamic occurs whether we are talking about "Moonies" and other quasi-Christian devotees or those involved in churches where servitude rather than servanthood is stressed. It is usually difficult to deprogram people who have been involved in cults because of the strength of the persons' beliefs and the guilt experienced by those being encouraged to leave. Entangled sexual and financial relationships are not uncommon. These relationships result in increased guilt and a need for these people who have been entrapped to learn basic trust again.

Counselors who work with people who have been caught in personality worship must be careful to develop basic trust with these people and not repeat the dependent relationships. The basic feelings of guilt will be overcome as they are able to begin to take charge of their own lives and rediscover basic beliefs and relationships.

One woman said, "I had lost sight of who I was as a wife and mother. My whole life was oriented toward my pastor. Before I could deal with my own guilt I had to come to grips with the fact that he too could be sinful and wrong."

I have found it helpful to direct such people to a study of the freedom that Christ intends believers to experience. If they can come to believe that he really does love them and accept them for who they are then they can follow the right Master and begin to use the gifts and abilities he has given them. There is no magic approach to life and there are no miracle workers of the kind the guru-followers seek. There is, however, a Savior, Christ the Lord, who said,

> Come to me, all you who are weary and burdened, and I will give you rest. Take my yoke upon you and learn from me, for I am gentle and humble in heart, and you will find rest for your souls. For my yoke is easy and my burden is light. (Matt. 11:28–30)

This same Jesus offered people freedom from their guilt and dependency by saying, "Go and sin no more. . . . Your sins are forgiven you."

In this chapter I have provided some examples which will enable the counselor to become aware of some of the types of relationships which may produce guilt. This awareness should be used to assist in carefully examining each counselee's individual situation. When relationships are guilt producing they need to be altered before the guilt can be released. This alteration may take the form of actual changes or by helping the person view the relationship differently. These changes in the way relationships are perceived can lead to new situations of freedom and to a reduction of the pain of guilt.

PART TWO

COUNSELING AND GUILT

CHAPTER NINE

COGNITIVE APPROACHES TO GUILT

WHEN PEOPLE ARE NOT THINKING CLEARLY they are usually not acting appropriately or feeling very stable. Confused thinking leads to inappropriate or ineffective behavior. This can be seen very clearly in relation to guilt.

Sam felt that he had to be loved by everyone. So, he would work overtime to try to gain the affection of those around him. In the process he would offend people and then the guilt would come flooding in. Sometimes the guilt was earned; at other times it was unearned. In either case his counselor needed to help him correct his thinking that seemed to get him into trouble with feelings of guilt.

Sam's counselor began to work on his cognitions (thoughts).

by having him look at the things he would tell himself about his situation. He shared three basic reactions which people have to situations—*catastrophizing, minimizing* or *being realistic.*

Watch for Catastrophizing

When you are dealing with unresolved guilt it is likely that the persons may be *catastrophizing* the situation. They may have accepted their behavior as sin, but they have continued to see the negative aspects of the sin in an exaggerated fashion. I often catastrophize when I am late for an appointment with one of my children. Instead of saying, *I am late,* I tell myself, *I am a bad parent.*

I am not saying that we should minimize sin, but what I am saying is that we need to teach our clients to tell it like it is and not continue to exaggerate the situation beyond what God or sound reason demands. It is no more virtuous to amplify the negative aspects of sin than it is to ignore such negative aspects. Both behavior patterns may keep us from breaking free from the clutches of guilt.

Minimizing Is Not the Answer

Minimizing a situation also contributes to problems of guilt because, invariably, it means that the person has denied or suppressed the facts. Confession, repentance, and the reception of forgiveness are impossible as long as the minimizing continues. People who deny or minimize still experience guilt. They just don't admit what it is that they feel guilty about.

In working with those who minimize I have found it helpful to focus on what they have done and not on the why. Asking why encourages people to excuse themselves. It also may increase confusion because they may not actually understand their motives. If motives are unclear, people may resort to a "devil-made-me-do-it" kind of attitude. By asking *what,* I allow them to deal with the facts of the situation whether the motives are known or not. Answering the what is usually sufficient to lead people to repentance and thus to the possibility of being released from their guilt.

Teach People to Stick with Reality

What do I mean by "sticking with reality"? I mean teaching people to tell themselves the truth, or at least as near as they can come to the truth. This reduces the sin or the situation to its lowest common denominator. When they tell themselves the truth they do not say that their sin had no consequence and neither do they say that it caused World War III or the famine in Africa.

Alan's sin of adultery had some very negative effects upon his family and the family of the woman involved. It was not, however, the cause of the fall in the stock market or the reason for his father's stroke. Until Alan was helped to stick with the reality of his sin he was unable to focus his attention where it needed to be—upon rebuilding his marriage. As long as he was ruminating about all the possible domino effects of what he had done he didn't face the issue nor did he receive release from the guilt he was feeling.

Becoming realistic about the situations for which people feel guilty may be made more difficult by the reactions of those around them. Generalized statements like "you have ruined my whole life" or "God has been disgraced" or "what will the Joneses think?" tend to take people's attention off the real issues of repentance, forgiveness, and getting on with life. When I deal with clients who are ruminating about all of the terrible side effects of what has happened I allow them to consider the extent of the situation—but at some point I begin to bring them back to the important issue. Alan needed to be helped to focus his attention on the aspects of the problem he could do something about and not continue to bounce back and forth between the real or imagined awful things outside of his control. Backward looks of remorse usually only keep guilt alive. They do not solve the problems created by the sin.

HELP PEOPLE EXAMINE THEIR BELIEFS

Another way to understand guilt is to help people understand their beliefs about the situation. For example, if a man who hurts another believes that the other deserved to be hurt he may minimize the situation and not confess his sin. On the other hand, if he believes that he himself is a bad person who always hurts others he may catastrophize himself into a deep depression that could continue long after the person whom he had hurt had extended forgiveness to him, and long after that person has forgotten that he said anything negative in the first place. This example shows how what we tell ourselves can affect the extent of guilt we feel—and our ability to gain release from guilt.

Dr. Albert Ellis has proposed a useful A B C D model for helping people understand themselves.[1] He points out that we usually view life as though something that happens to us (A) leads to a specific consequence (C). For example, if my wife refuses to kiss me (A) I may believe that that leads to (C) my feeling bad. However, this is not necessarily true because what I believe about the situation (B) may radically change the meaning which the event has for me. If I believe my wife has a cold, the resulting (C) might be that I feel even more loved. I tell myself: *she loves me so much that she would turn down the ecstasy of my kiss in order to protect me from the discomfort of a cold.*

On the other hand, if I believe that she doesn't find me very sexually attractive (B2) then I may feel depressed or angry. This illustration points out that there is no direct connection between A (starting events) and C (consequences). The connection is people's beliefs (B) about the particular situation. Consequences are very much affected by the beliefs and evaluations we attach to a given situation.

What people believe about a particular situation which may produce guilt will also determine the ultimate effect the guilt may have upon them. Sally desired to remain a virgin until she married. She had worked hard to control her passions so that she would reach this goal. Her very strict parents had tried to motivate her toward sexual purity by telling her how bad it would be if she engaged in premarital sex. They used fear tactics and even implied that they wouldn't love her as much if she lost her virginity. As a result, Sally was constantly tense and hard on herself anytime she would think about sex. Sally and Phillip became engaged and planned a wedding in the near future. However, one night their sexual desires got out of hand and they made love. The next day Sally's world began to fall apart. Look at the A B Cs of her life as shown in this illustration.

A	B	C
Having Premarital Sex	B1 "I have done the worst thing I could do."	Guilt
	B2 "My life can never be happy now."	Depression
	B3 "I have disgraced my parents."	Withdrawal
	B4 "I have ruined Phillip's life."	Self-punishment
	B5 "I am a horrible person."	
	B6 "I don't deserve to live."	

Sally's Negative Beliefs Following Sin

You can readily see from the diagram that the beliefs Sally had about her behavior produced an array of negative emotions. Indeed, she was at the very point of suicide. As her counselor, I had to help her realize that there were other ways to view the situation. These options are presented below.

A	B	C
Having Premarital Sex	B1 "What I did was wrong."	Remorse
	B2 "I need to seek forgiveness."	Sadness
	B3 "Phillip and I still love each other very much."	Joy with forgiveness
	B4 "My parents are hurt but they will get over it."	Resolve to have better self-control
	B5 "God has forgiven me."	Getting on with life
	B6 "I am no less of a person than I was."	

Sally's Realistic Beliefs Following Sin

You can see by comparing the two that the belief system through which Sally processed her behavior made all the difference in the world. It is possible that had she adhered to negative beliefs Sally would have remained depressed and suicidal and might never have become free from her guilt. She would feel too hopeless to receive forgiveness. However, by holding to realistic beliefs she would still feel badly, but she would seek and find the forgiveness she needed.

The role of the counselor who uses this system is to help people tell themselves the truth and to bring the positive truths of Scripture and of their circumstances to bear on the problem. Sally's parents had programed her to focus upon the worst possible thing that could happen and without help she would probably have taken her life. The theology was wrong (God does forgive) and the psychology was wrong (a single sin need not destroy one's life). It took time to walk Sally through this process because her parental programing did not die easily, but after a time, she began to consider the other possibilities and was able to be free of her guilt.

Teach People to Think Correctly

Thus far we have not discussed the fourth aspect of the Ellis model, disputing or substituting beliefs, the process represented by the letter "D" (for disrupting). Many beliefs that clients have are either false or irrational. It is the counselor's job to help the client evaluate these beliefs and either substitute new, more appropriate ones or to learn to dispute the irrational beliefs so that the negative consequences will not be realized.

We will use Sally's negative belief B4 as an example. Most would agree that it is irrational to believe that Sally had "ruined Phillip's life." The counselor may wish to consider several issues in beginning to dispute Sally's belief: Did she make Phillip have sex or did he participate in it willingly? Is there any evidence that Phillip's life will be ruined? Is it possible for him to be forgiven by God, by his family, and even by her? Does Phillip feel that his life has been ruined? Will this act prevent the two of them from being married? And if so, what basis does she have for believing that they are doomed to unhappiness because of one sexual indiscretion?

Without giving a verbatim account of how the disputing process proceeded, it is enough to say that as Sally was slowly and sensitively brought to think critically about her stated belief, it began to weaken. I helped her by affirming that she may feel like all of life—Phillip's and hers—was ruined, though there was no evidence of that being so.

Another vital part of the disputing was to help her realize that part of what she was experiencing was fear. She feared that Phillip's life might be ruined, which, of course, meant that her life would be adversely affected also. As she came to realize that her extreme fears were unfounded the panic lessened and she gained a greater willingness to look at the situation more realistically.

After Sally had come to the point of acknowledging that what she had been saying to herself was not true, I asked her to formulate a more realistic response. She finally was able to say, "Phillip's life could be hurt by what I did, but I sure hope it won't." Later on she was able to go a step further and say, "We will have to work at rebuilding trust with our parents, but we should be successful because all in all we have been very trustworthy." By this point Sally was well on the way to accepting the joy of forgiveness and giving up her guilt.

One further comment needs to be made about the type of irrational belief Sally was carrying. The focus of her concern over the possibility of a ruined life was upon Phillip; she had said little about concerns for herself. This made me suspicious. I wondered about projection. Was it possible that the anger she felt toward herself for ruining Phillip's life might have been a cover-up for some feelings of anger she had toward Phillip for his part in putting her life in jeopardy? As Sally's understanding of herself increased I was able to approach this sensitive area and help her work through her negative feelings toward Phillip. If this had not been uncovered it is highly likely that her resentment would have continued to grow, and more and more feelings of guilt would have resulted. As Sally became aware of these negative feelings that had developed, I encouraged her to confess them to Phillip. As the two of them talked, Phillip also confessed what he considered his wrongdoing to Sally. This maximized the release from guilt on both their parts and sent them into their marriage mostly healed and ready to proceed with the process of making a good life together. It is hard to say what would have happened if they had not received therapy and if Sally's irrational beliefs had not been disputed. What we can say with a high degree of certainty is that the healing process was speeded up and the anguish was cut to a minimum.

Watch for a Repeat Performance

When I work with clients who have guilt feelings I usually assume that the difficulties they are having over situations of the moment will probably repeat themselves. It is crucial therefore to teach people the process of telling themselves the truth and disputing the negative beliefs that tend to hinder release from the guilt. Teaching people these cognitive skills is a good way to increase their confidence and thereby increase their feelings of self-worth. Learning new skills is an essential factor in being able to avoid previous failures.

The apostle Paul taught that the result of right thinking will be peace from God. Is there anything that guilt-ridden clients need more?

Finally, brothers, whatever is true, whatever is noble, whatever is right, whatever is pure, whatever is lovely, whatever is admirable—if anything is excellent or praiseworthy—think about such things. Whatever you have learned or received or heard from me, or seen in me— put it into practice. And the God of peace will be with you.   (Phili. 4:8, 9).

Reframing

Another important cognitive skill to master in helping guilt-ridden clients is called *reframing.* This activity, as one might guess, means to look at the problem or situation from a different perspective. Two illustrations should help you grasp this important counseling tool.

Millie came to see me because she was plagued with fears. She was afraid to go to church, afraid of the people at work, and even afraid to be alone with her children. She was plagued by unearned guilt which was reinforced by her fears. She interpreted her fear as guilt. "I must be a bad person to feel this way. I must have done something wrong."

There were three important steps involved in teaching Millie to reframe her thoughts.

First, she had to be taught to become more aware of the signals coming from her body. Often she would not realize that she was upset until she had become angry with others or was slumped over with depression. Tight muscles, headaches, stomach aches, excessive tiredness, or shakiness all may have been signs of tension which, in turn, may have been the result of nonproductive thinking. Millie needed to become aware of this process so that she could take better control of her life.

131

Secondly, Millie had to learn to reframe her thoughts, especially those that were irrational. She needed to specify what she was saying about herself and what she was saying about various aspects of her circumstances. Those clarifications helped her to better understand and control her guilt.

Thirdly, she had to learn to reinterpret her situation from a different perspective. She needed to change her view just as an old picture can be taken out of a frame and replaced with a new one.

Here is how the process worked for Millie. When she began to be fearful she felt a tenseness in her abdomen. As she learned to recognize this body signal she often discovered that she was saying something to herself like: *I'm probably going to die. I can't control this pressure. I must have done something bad.*

I taught Millie to reframe by asking herself, "What is another interpretation I could give for what is going on with me?" At first this was awkward, but she did it consistently and she learned quickly. She gave herself a reframed answer such as, "I've felt this way before and I didn't die. God is with me and he promised to protect me. I can't think of anything I have done wrong so I must just be down on myself."

The more she practiced this reframing the more automatic it became and the more quickly she was able to bring her fears under control. Notice that reframing was used as a process by which Millie could confront her false guilt. This is very important for highly anxious people because they will tend to interpret most body signals from a guilt perspective and in the process they may become so preoccupied with their anxious, guilty feelings that they don't deal with earned guilt when it occurs. Anxiety can become a substitute for dealing with sin. Later on in Millie's treatment I was able to help her go back and reframe some of the guilt-producing statements from her past and thus defuse their destructive potential in the here and now. Dealing with the carry-overs from the past frees people to deal with the present from a realistic point of view.

Reframing from a Biblical Perspective

Nick is an example of one whose reframing needed to be done from a biblical or religious perspective. He tended to support most of his guilty feelings with what he thought scriptural truth to be, or "the way God is." When Nick would say, "That's what the Bible says," I would force reframing by asking, "What else could that mean?" or "Do you think God treats everyone that way or just you?" Later on in the treatment process I was able to help him reexamine his view of God and to expand it to include God's willingness to love us and forgive us. This type of reframing was essential in helping him deal with his guilt. When he would frame a situation from his narrow, negative view, I taught him to ask himself, "What would your new, broader view of God say about the situation?"

Pamela Butler points out how negative views are often acquired and maintained:

> Our unquestioning acceptance of negative judgments also results from the fact that significant others in our pasts have frequently failed to oppose our negative self-talk. During childhood, negative messages were perhaps reinforced by many people and many experiences. As we grew up, we continued to surround ourselves with individuals who were not supportive, or we did not put our negative beliefs to a test. By not revealing them to anyone, we had little chance of correcting our harsh self-judgments, even if the current environment was itself very positive.[2]

Reframing requires the therapist to become keenly aware of the perspectives from which counselees approach life and then call upon biblical truth and psychological realities to equip these people to gain new hope for their lives. I have found that good questions are an invaluable asset in helping people examine their religious beliefs and reframe those that are not based upon sound biblical interpretation. Questions, such as "what are some of the Scriptures your view is based upon?" or "how do you feel this relates to other Bible teaching?" seem to force people to examine their beliefs and be ready for reframed truth.

On your own, apart from your actual counseling, you may wish to practice reframing and other tools presented in this book in order to gain the confidence necessary for using them with guilt-ridden counselees. After you have learned the skills, teach them to your counselees and have them practice the skills with you in your office. Don't assume that they know the skills simply as a result of your explanation. You may be a good teacher, but don't take the risk of being misunderstood.

DIRECT TEACHING

Any discussion of cognitive approaches for dealing with guilt would be incomplete without including the direct teaching methods. Many people who are wrestling with guilt will not find release until they find God and/or discover the truth from Scripture that can serve to guide them to guilt-free living. Just as people must be taught to think rationally (tell themselves the truth) they must also be taught to think biblically (in line with the Bible's truth). Having learned biblical truth, people can then be encouraged to change some of the guilt-producing patterns their lives are following.

When I am presented with a problem by a client I usually ask, "Do you have a personal faith or any religious beliefs which might be a resource to you in dealing with this problem?"

This simple question allows me to find out whether or not people are believers. If they are believers I might ask, "What do you feel God's perspective is on your situation?" If they do not know, I may ask if they would like to learn. If they say yes, I have three options: teach them during the sessions, give them homework to help them discover it for themselves, or send them to their pastor or a Bible teacher in whom I have confidence. If in my judgment their view of God's perspective is wrong, I have the same three options to use in correcting the error. The important thing is not how it is done but *that* it is done. I believe counselors shy away too much from helping people understand how the Bible relates to their lives.

If the client is a nonbeliever I might share my perspective that the only cure for guilt is forgiveness and that I believe in a personal God who stands ready and willing to forgive. I usually ask if that is a new concept and if so, would he or she like to learn more about it. If the answer is yes, I can exercise options presented above or I can tell him or her I would be happy to talk about it on my time. As a Christian therapist I feel strongly that I should not use my position as a platform for indoctrination. But I also feel I must be true to myself and my God in offering the Christian option to those who have not considered it. If my client has earned guilt, he or she needs to know that forgiveness is possible on both a human and a divine level. Unlike some who feel that they should not counsel a person who refuses to become a Christian, I believe in continuing to work with the person to offer whatever help is possible even if the ultimate basis for a solution to the problem is rejected. My friendship and concern may serve as the bridge to a Christian experience at a later time.

In short, then, there are times in which direct teaching is not only appropriate but essential. My friend and colleague, Dr. DeLoss Friesen, defines counseling as highly specialized one-on-one teaching. I accept this definition and strive to be the best teacher I can be for each client I serve. I urge counselors not to rely strictly on group teaching skills. Learn all you can about teaching one on one. More talk is probably not the answer.

BIBLICAL COUNSELING

The biblical counseling view of Dr. Lawrence Crabb deserves special mention as a cognitive approach that carefully integrates biblical and psychological principles. His model of counseling is shown in the following chart which appears in one of his books.[3]

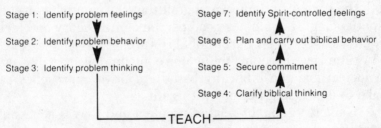

STAGES OF COUNSELING

Stage 1: Identify problem feelings

Stage 2: Identify problem behavior

Stage 3: Identify problem thinking

Stage 7: Identify Spirit-controlled feelings

Stage 6: Plan and carry out biblical behavior

Stage 5: Secure commitment

Stage 4: Clarify biblical thinking

TEACH

The elements of the model need to be underscored. Stages one through three emphasize understanding the problem from three perspectives: feelings, behavior, and thinking.

Then the key element comes—"teach." This is followed by, or integrated with, clarification, securing commitment, planning, and getting the person to act on biblical principles. The process is not complete, however, until stage 7. The counselee needs to identify Spirit-controlled feelings which serve to equip him or her to better deal with new problems or issues that may arise.

Crabb gives four suggestions for helping change wrong thinking to right thinking. These are included here in abbreviated form as an encouragement to the reader to further explore his system.

1. Identify where the wrong assumption was learned. People relearn best when they can clearly see where the original error may have happened.

2. Encourage expression of emotion around the belief. When people talk about their feelings the counselor can better judge how attached they are to the incorrect beliefs that are causing them trouble.

3. Support the counselee as he or she considers changing assumptions. It is much easier to consider changing than to change. The counselee will need your encouragement and gentle nudge toward action.

4. Teach the counselee what to fill his or her mind with; the "Tape Recorder" technique (repeating over and over the true or preferred thoughts). Deliberate action is needed. This cannot be left to chance.

I believe this approach is particularly relevant to problems of guilt because it allows for one integrated approach to deal with both the earned and unearned guilt that the counselee may be experiencing. It combines good psychological theory and technique with the freeing truth of Scripture.

In summary, here are the major contributions that the psychological and the biblically based cognitive approaches can make to counseling persons with guilt.

1. Guilt is a thought-related problem and thus is accessible to treatment via the thinking channel.

2. Cognitive analysis of guilt can help both counselee and therapist better understand the problem and thus attack it together.

3. The cognitive approach can be integrated with other approaches that might be helpful in dealing with the affective aspects of guilt.

4. The cognitive approach is consistent with the biblical injunctions related to the importance of right thinking.

5. The cognitive approach takes away the mystique of the therapist and gives the clients the responsibility they need to have.

6. The cognitive approach is easily understood and learned by most clients.

7. The cognitive approach is easily learned by most therapists without having to understand a plethora of other psychological theories.

CHAPTER TEN

SELF-DISCOVERY APPROACHES TO GUILT

WHEN A PERSON SUFFERING FROM GUILT approaches a counselor, the counselor is often tempted to take charge. Cliff said, "My counselor told me what was wrong with me and he told me what to do about it. When I got home from meeting with him I realized that I was just as confused as ever. He didn't tell me a thing I didn't already know."

When people are given advice or treated to interpretations of their behavior which may not be accurate, the result is usually more confusion and more guilt. Proper solutions do no good unless the counselees are able to integrate them into their thoughts, feelings, and behaviors. One approach to helping counselees accomplish this is the nondirective or self-discovery approach.

A pioneer in the self-discovery area was Carl R. Rogers who developed the client-centered approach to counseling. The emphasis of this approach is upon the relationship between the counselor and the counselee. Through this relationship the counselee is helped to discover what Rogers called "the fully functioning person." Regarding the type of relationship that is most helpful in the client-centered process, Patterson writes,

> The relationship that the counselor provides for the client is not an intellectual relationship. The counselor cannot help the client by his knowledge. Explaining the client's personality and behavior to him and prescribing actions that he should take are of little lasting value. The relationship that is helpful to the client, that enables him to discover within himself the capacity to use that relationship to change and grow, is not a cognitive, intellectual one.[1]

The Rogerian approach has been criticized by some authors on theological grounds (it is based on the notion of human goodness and the ability to improve ourselves with or without God) and practical grounds (it sometimes leaves people confused and floundering). Yet the theory needs to be examined carefully to evaluate what it has to offer with regard to helping people who are struggling with guilt. In this chapter several positive contributions of self-discovery approaches will be discussed and then some of the negative implications or drawbacks will be outlined.

POSITIVE CONTRIBUTIONS OF SELF-DISCOVERY APPROACHES

When you are dealing with guilt you are dealing with both thoughts and feelings, and the feelings may be compounded by the thoughts. Counselors often assume that this dilemma can be solved by new information. Thus Scripture is quoted or interpretations or observations of the counselor are offered. These well-meaning attempts may be less than helpful, however, if they do not fit the situation or if their implementation is surrounded by confusion, or what I have referred to earlier as compacted feelings. In client-centered therapy the counselor does not tell but asks and reflects the feelings he or she hears coming from the client. For example, the counselor might say, "You are feeling confused and helpless. You feel like you have done something so bad that no one could ever forgive you."

"That's right," the counselee might respond. "I don't even know if I can forgive myself." After a reflective silence the counselor might say,

"Help me to understand that better. I want to know what all this really means to you."

Bringing Feelings into Awareness

The result of such an exchange would be a loosening of feelings on the part of the counselees. Through the process of expressing the feelings in an accepting, nonthreatening environment, counselees become less afraid of the feelings and may be able to look at them from a new perspective. As the counselor reflects back or restates what he or she hears, they may become aware of feelings that were pressed down so tightly they were beyond their awareness.

Merrill's counselor clenched his fists at his sides, gritted his teeth, and yelled, "I'm just so angry I can hardly stand it." Merrill sat stunned for a while and then said, "I didn't realize until you yelled that that is exactly how I am feeling."

Loosening up feelings is a process that cannot be rushed. The self-discovery approaches such as client-centered counseling let the counselee do most of the talking. Counselees will get to what they want to say in their own time. I have often encouraged them to slow down. "We don't have to solve anything today." I have said, "Let's just talk about those feelings. It may be helpful for you to see me as a mirror. I'll reflect some feelings back to you and you may be able to understand yourself better. You'll do a lot better in dealing with your guilt when you can separate out some of the feelings that are there."

As my counselee did relax and verbalize some of those feelings he said, "There is so much there that I haven't even realized before. I could have gone right past it all."

Progress through Careful Pacing

Proper pacing is the key to working through feelings. The self-discovery approaches are a way of assisting counselees in experiencing their world in new ways. Guilt, for example, is often accompanied by panic or self-destructiveness such as physically hurting one's self or saying things that damage relationships. The counselor's calmness and lack of alarm may help the counselee to discover that he or she can view the problem in a similar calm, rational manner.

"When I told my counselor all my ugly feelings and she didn't get all upset or tell me what to do I began to feel like I might be able to deal with the situation after all," Judy said. "The more I felt this the more I opened up to the counselor and to myself. I guess I wasn't panicked anymore."

Guilt is often experienced as a phenomenon of the past, although it is directly affecting the client in the present. As long as it is experienced in this way little relief will be seen. Through self-discovery, persons may realize what they are doing to themselves or what they are doing to others right now.

Power to Deal with the Present

Walter said, "As I talked I realized I had to stop thinking about the past. I couldn't change a thing about that. What I had to do was get me where I needed to be right now. As I did this my guilt began to subside. My problem wasn't what I had done—it was what I was doing. I was copping out on life and blaming it on my guilty feelings over my sin."

When problems are experienced externally, as outside the person, they will not be productively addressed. However, as the counselor listens, understands the counselee, and empathically communicates that understanding and acceptance, the counselee can begin to perceive the situation from an internal perspective.

Melissa said, "When I realized it was within me rather than something outside, I realized that God was in me too and between the two of us we could do something besides wallow in the guilt."

Counselee Self-Understanding Grows

Another change that often takes place through the self-discovery approaches is that the counselees begin to "get it together." They feel less fragmented as their feelings become better understood. In the process their experience of guilt begins to change. Melissa went on to say, "I didn't feel like two persons anymore—a nice person and an ugly one. I felt like a nice person who had done some ugly things but could be forgiven. I had become almost paranoid because I felt like people could look right into my heart and see all the evil."

I have discussed the importance of uniting various aspects of our thoughts and feelings. I believe that congruence is a necessary step to freedom from guilt. Contradictions exist within all people, but they cannot be resolved until they are accepted by the persons as belonging to them. Once the contradictions are acknowledged counselees are free to ask, "What do I want to do about this?"

Denial Is Weakened

Denial is often very strong for those persons who experience guilt over sexual feelings. They will even go so far as to shut out that area of their lives completely.

Beth said, "I couldn't even let myself admit that I had sexual feelings. They were only blurred, dark shadows that crossed my confused mind. One day during a counseling session you referred to a person who had sexual thoughts and I realized I had denied that category also. I knew that I had denied my sexuality because I was afraid I couldn't control it. As you let me talk and my feelings became more clear I realized that I had spent a lot of time feeling guilty when I didn't have to. The word normal was a great help the first time I was able to use it when referring to myself."

Interestingly enough, Beth did lose control and sinned sexually but she was able to receive forgiveness, forgive herself and go on with life because she was recognizing the problem as hers. You cannot receive relief from guilt until you acknowledge that it is a part of you.

143

Freedom from Secrets

Individuals who suffer from guilt spend much of their time and emotional energy hiding. Keeping secrets is a very costly thing to do emotionally. I had spent several sessions listening to Ron and watching him grow in his confidence in me and in himself. He finally took the risk of sharing some of his secrets and it was as if a great weight had been lifted. I had reflected his fears and his anxiety and he was beginning to understand which ones made sense and which ones did not. One day he came in and said, "I made a big decision this week. I'm going to tell my dad about the money I took. I don't know whether he will be able to forgive me or not but I realized over the weekend that if he doesn't, we won't be any further apart than we are due to my guilt and avoiding him. At least he will understand why and I won't have to keep this awful secret anymore."

The insights and courage Ron had gained through the self-discovery aspect of counseling had brought him to a place of action—action which could lead to freedom from guilt. After the confrontation with his dad had taken place and things had settled down, I asked him if anyone had ever told him that he needed to talk to his father. His reply was revealing.

"Lots of times," he said. "But I'm not sure I could ever hear it until I said it to myself." Ron, like many, had not been able to take action as a result of being told what to do. Through the less directive counseling approach he had discovered what he wanted to do. Individuals will only take responsibility for their behavior when they feel confident enough in their self-understanding to feel that it can turn out okay. This leads to decisive action. The acceptance and support of the counselor may facilitate such action.

Ron said, "I guess I knew that even if the bottom fell out with Dad you would stick with me until I could regroup."

Leaving Fears Behind

The ability of counselees to communicate regarding themselves to others in a specific environment may not always be present. Have you ever had a counselee say, "But they wouldn't understand"? Such a remark is not aimed at the listener but at the communicator himself. I asked Emily if she thought anyone could help her husband understand her feelings. After pondering the question she said, "I think you might be able to." We realized that Emily's real concern was that she would not be able to express herself when her husband began to pressure her. The more I allowed her to talk and the less I took responsibility for her communication within the counseling session the more confidence she developed in her ability to express herself. We discovered that some of her guilt was not for what she had done. She felt inadequate about her ability to deal with the situation with her husband. The self-discovery approach gave her the opportunity she needed to develop expressive skills and eventually to sort out her earned guilt from what was unearned. When the sorting process was complete she was able to deal with each appropriately and leave them behind.

New Ways to Think

Another positive aspect of the self-discovery approaches is that many people begin to change how they think about themselves and their world. People live their lives on the basis of assumptions made about how things will happen, how people will react, or even how God will respond to them. Many times any resemblance to reality is purely coincidental. Unearned guilt and fear are often the products of people's assumptions. They believe that they should behave in certain ways because of the way they perceive their world. When their behavior does not match up to their expectations or what they feel others expect of them, feelings of guilt often result. Faulty assumptions about expectations often go on and on for years before they are tested. People struggle under the guilt but are unable to challenge the assumptions that have produced it because "that's just the way things are." I call this playing the ball game before going to the ball park.

The more counselees are able to express themselves the more likely they are to discover their wrong perceptions or assumptions. If the counselor does not put counselees on the defensive they may discover that their views of the world are incorrect. Remember, errors in perception are not corrected by logic or argumentation. They are corrected by self-discovery. For example, when a question arises about how long it takes to walk to the grocery store people will hold firmly to their beliefs until they actually observe the time for themselves. Being told they are wrong won't change their minds.

It is wonderful to hear a counselee say, "I have been looking at this all wrong." Sometimes credit is given to the counselor when all he or she has done is allow the counselee to listen to his or her own ideas in an environment where a lot of energy isn't invested in protecting those ideas. Larry said, "When my counselor didn't put my ideas down somehow I began to be more self-critical and I realized that some of my thoughts didn't hold water."

When counselees are making faulty generalizations the counselor may probe by saying, "I need to know how you are relating these two situations." Usually this question is adequate to help them discover the errors in their thinking. As Nate tried to explain, he said, "That really doesn't fit, does it? I'm feeling guilty because I fear abandoning my wife the way my father did my mother—and I'm really not acting like Dad at all." The self-discovery environment had enabled him to correct some pieces in his troubled cognitive map.

Persons who struggle with guilt often have their world tightly tied together in order to protect themselves. They can't stand loopholes or looseness because that might result in even more bad feelings. In their self-protective zeal they often create traps from which they cannot escape. Nondirective or client-centered approaches often create the atmosphere in which the person can discover the ways in which the attempts to tie everything up tightly may have actually created the problem rather than provided a solution.

Stefanie was so afraid of failing that she set extremely high standards, and then she forced herself to believe and act as though she had no value unless she met those standards.

One day I asked, "Who are the people that feel you have no value unless you accomplish all these things?"

She burst into tears: "I guess I'm the only one. I've been so

146

afraid of not being accepted that I have created demands for myself that I just couldn't meet." After a silence she continued, "The problem now is that I don't know how to reverse that. I don't have a world in which I can survive."

At this point I had to bite my tongue. I had identified with her pain and wanted so much to provide her with quick relief. I wanted to answer her question and tell her how it could all be okay. Experience has taught me, however, that this never works. The persons who bind themselves with tight mental chains are invariably the persons who must learn for themselves how to loosen them. I forced myself to allow Stefanie to ponder her dilemma. Her mind began to work along with her tear ducts. For a moment it was as though I had left the room. She cried and talked to herself. She wiped her tears and talked some more. She needed me to be there; she didn't need my advice. I knew that there would be time later for me to provide input or to ask questions which she may have overlooked.

Sometimes world views must be shattered and pet perceptions must be strewn around the room before the counselees can understand themselves and/or their guilt enough to move ahead with their lives. It is sometimes comfortable for them to feel that their lives are all neatly packaged. But the reality is often that the life and the package don't fit. At this point, self-discovery techniques are marvelous tools.

New Ways of Handling Problems

Self-discovery approaches may also help people learn to relate to their problems differently. Bart said, "I know I'm going at this all wrong but for the life of me I can't figure out how." Instead of trying to provide answers for a situation the counselor couldn't possibly know well enough to understand, she simply said, "I sense your anguish and your strong desire to get this all behind you." Bart nodded affirmatively and began to launch out in that direction.

I always assume that if people knew how to solve their problems they would have done it. Although this is not always true, it is a good place to start. I further assume that the solutions that counselees discover for themselves are usually the solutions that have the greatest likelihood of implementation. Creative problem-solving is usually stymied by continued wrestling with guilt. The goal of the self-discovery approach is to provide the environment in which this ability to relate to the problem in new, more creative ways may be restored. By refusing to tell Bart how to do things right, Bart's counselor helped him find new ways of approaching the situation. She let him stew but she didn't let him burn. In essence, her acceptance of him and his problem encouraged him to try another way. Sometimes they were old ways that needed to be tried again, such as "talk to God about it." Other times they were new ways that Bart had not conceived when he was under the pressure to do it right. After most of his counseling was complete, Bart told a friend, "The thing that probably helped me the most was her willingness to let me tread water until I could learn how to swim again. I stopped seeing myself as the problem and realized it was time to grab hold of some solutions. The guilt was still there but now I had it labeled 'S' for solvable."

With increased confidence in one's ability to approach problems come new possibilities in relating. Becky had to learn to relate person to person. She had always put her guilt, most of which was unearned, between herself and the other individual. Her guilt was a shroud which covered her identity.

"I wouldn't let them see who I am," she said. "I was afraid they wouldn't accept what they saw and I had little confidence in my ability to change if they didn't like me." Becky took some risks in the way she related to her counselor and eventually she began to relate to others differently as well.

"It's hard to break old habits," she said, "but I'm making it."

One of the most predictable results of guilt is that it destroys relationships and regresses relational skills. People who struggle with guilt struggle with people. No matter how well they relate they usually feel that they have destroyed or will destroy their relationships. Feelings of unworthiness do destroy spontaneity, and without spontaneity and honesty relationships wither. As counselees begin to realize that they are able to relate to a counselor they may begin to open up to the possibility of relating to others as well. This will not happen if the counselor has done all the talking. The lecture method is never an effective way of teaching communication skills and it proves to be just as ineffective in getting people past guilt and back to healthy relationships. Being an expert is always tempting but not usually very helpful.

Self-discovery methods are not adequate in and of themselves to help people develop relational skills, but they do pave the way for a willingness to learn more.

Becky said, "I've learned how to talk to you pretty well. I stumble around but I get there. I feel like I need to approach people more. Do you have any books that will help?" Becky's road to recovery was now being paved and she was becoming the major contractor. The residual guilt feelings that follow confession and forgiveness have trouble existing in the face of success. Becky went from the tunnel vision of guilt and isolation to the broad horizons of freedom, self-confidence, and new relationships.

Each positive aspect of a client-centered or self-discovery approach may be used in combination with other interventions. I see them as basic to the establishment of an atmosphere where other approaches can also be used. Counselors who fail in their use of these methods, or others for that matter, usually fail because they are focusing on the method and not on the unique needs or qualities of the counselee.

NEGATIVE ASPECTS OF SELF-DISCOVERY APPROACHES

Any approach to change is only as stable as the assumptions upon which it is based. Self-discovery approaches are vulnerable at this point because they are often based upon the assumption that human beings have the capacity within themselves to do right or what is in their own best interests.

Sometimes this is just not the case. World wars and personal disasters have shown us that people aren't getting better and better. In fact, the current threat of nuclear holocaust stands as a gigantic warning of mankind's great capacity to self-destruct, on both an individual and a societal basis. The counselor dare not take the responsibility for life away from the counselee but he or she must also remain constantly alert to the potential of the client to make bad choices or to in other ways contribute to the problem rather than the solution.

I do not believe that client-centered or self-discovery approaches should be dismissed on theological grounds. I do, however, believe that the approaches may be based on half truths which must be constantly monitored. For example, people are capable of learning helpful things about themselves. Even evil men do improve themselves and their situations through careful introspection. They do not, however, come to a place of saving themselves. Regardless of the self-improvement they still need God in their lives. Self-discovery or self-improvement is not a substitute for salvation. Yet even this truth must often be self-discovered or taught by the quiet voice of Scripture when coupled with the convincing power of the Holy Spirit. I believe the Holy Spirit can use me as a counselor just as powerfully when I listen as when I may speak. In fact, sometimes words get in the way. I have chosen, therefore, not to discard self-discovery techniques but rather to recognize the limitations of the assumptions on which they are based and to proceed from there with proper caution.

A second caution to be observed with self-discovery approaches is that for some immobilized clients they may not offer enough direction to get them started. Herb is a good example. He was able to talk some about his feelings, but his fears seemed to get in the way of greater self-understanding or progress toward leaving his guilt behind. He needed models to follow and sometimes he was best helped by direct assignments that forced him to see his problems differently. Herb's counselor forced him into a situation where he had to talk to a friend he had offended. He later said, "I would never have done that on my own but I now see how important it was."

The counselor must always exercise discernment not to do things for people that they can do for themselves, or to tell them things they can discover for themselves. However, there are times when without nudging the person will not grow.

Even when people are not immobilized emotionally they may have beliefs or behaviors that prevent them from continuing to progress along the self-discovery lines. In these cases the counselor needs to maintain the relationship and the accepting atmosphere while teaching the new beliefs or behaviors that are compatible with continued growth. Cognitive and/or behavioral approaches may be very helpful at this point. In other instances, it may be necessary to go back to periods of time in the person's life which may have been repressed or to work through personality distractions or problems of character. In such instances the more directive approaches may be called for. Effective counselors usually have more than one tool in their tool case.

Potential for Inefficiency

Another negative aspect of self-discovery approaches is the potential for inefficiency. A counselee who had seen a client-centered pastoral counselor complained, "We made some progress, but it took ten times as long as it should have. There were times when I became angry because I felt like he knew where I needed to be going but refused to tell me. I think I would have liked it better if he had directed me more but still had allowed me to make the final decisions about what was best for me. I spent time with him that I could have used in solving the problem."

Obviously there is a delicate balance here. When counselees are directed too much they don't learn very quickly nor is the result a permanent one, and the ultimate result is inefficiency. On the other hand, when they are left to flounder and discover steps by themselves that could easily be outlined by the counselor, efficiency is also lost. The solution is most likely to be found in knowing the counselees and how they learn best. As a counselor you always have the option of redirecting the session when things are not progressing at the pace you feel they should.

A graduate student whom I was supervising said, "I think I made a mistake with my client today. I gave her so much direction I don't think she will believe she can carry it out. If she can't, I know she will eventually drop out."

"What can you do about it?" I asked.

"If it was a mistake and she can't handle it then I will have to tell her so," he replied. As was suspected, the client didn't follow through and called to cancel the session. The student happened to answer the telephone and confessed his error. The client ended up keeping the appointment and the counselor played much more of a supportive, client-centered role with her. The outcome was successful.

It is important to remember that you only make mistakes when you fail to realize the impact of your behavior or decisions on the client. Look for the most efficient methods but be patient enough to acknowledge that you can't treat everyone in the same way. Some people's problems with guilt come and go quickly; others require much more patience and flexibility on the part of the counselor.

Finally, self-discovery approaches may be negative when they result in a general lack of direction for the counseling session. I have found it helpful to assist clients in developing a road map of steps or experiences that may take them from the valley of guilt to the plains of productivity. Some clients have the background or experience to discover these steps and take them. Others are so confused or inexperienced that they are almost incapable of seeing the steps even if you point them out. I usually say to counselees as I finish each session, "Here are some steps that I heard you say you would like to be able to take" (assuming that I heard some). "You might also want to think about doing _____ . Is this a direction you feel you are capable of going?"

Having a plan develops confidence. Too much dependence on self-discovery can undermine the confidence of the counselee in the counseling process. Even if the counselor relies heavily on self-discovery it is usually beneficial to help the counselee order his or her discoveries so that they have an even greater sense of direction.

Self-discovery methods, like all other approaches, need to be carefully monitored so that they best meet the needs of the client. There are both positives and negatives to be considered so that the counselees can be helped slowly but surely toward freedom from their guilt.

CHAPTER ELEVEN

DYNAMIC APPROACHES TO GUILT

CONSCIENTIOUS COUNSELORS are constantly asking themselves questions about what they are doing. They want to do it right. They want to understand the most helpful ways to intervene with people so that they can help as many people as possible. One question that usually arises is "do I have to deal with the counselee's past?" Stated differently, it might be "can I deal with the client in the here and now? Was Freud right? Is the pattern of feeling guilty fixed by age seven?"

The issue is more than academic because if human problems such as guilt have their mooring in the early childhood experiences, then to treat the present while ignoring the past may be doomed to failure.

It is also true that what counselees believe about themselves will control their responses to your attempts to help. If, for example, counselees believe that they are bad because they had bad parents, and because of the way their parents treated them, you will only fail if you try to do all your work in the here and now. You defeat yourself if, by the direction of your counseling, you go against the counselees' beliefs that they must understand their background in order to change.

Tim was suffering from a phobia that is usually best treated by dealing with the here and now and by prescribing a confrontation with the fear. I have successfully used this approach many times, but in Tim's case it did not work. I was baffled until I finally discussed the situation with him, and then I discovered that he didn't believe he could be helped without dealing with his childhood. The mystery was solved. We talked about his past and then he had confidence in the approach I was suggesting, and he improved dramatically.

In addition to dealing with the past out of *necessity*, we should recognize that some therapies that emphasize the importance of the past offer significant contributions to those who counsel with regard to guilt. What, for example, do Freud and his colleagues have to offer?

POSITIVE CONTRIBUTIONS OF DYNAMICALLY ORIENTED COUNSELING

The term *dynamic* or *psychodynamic* refers to the effects significant relationships have upon a person's experiences during the process of growing up. Freud referred to stages of psychosexual development or periods of time and experiences which have a dynamic effect upon the personality growth of the individual. Awareness of one's body and body functions and identification with or attachment to parents all have significant effect upon the way persons see themselves and their world. The way persons come to view their sexuality, for example, will have a great deal to do with the way they are affected by guilt, earned or unearned.

Lu Ann was experiencing guilt over having sex even though she was married and had never had sex with anyone but her husband, and that after marriage. In searching for the reason, we went back to her childhood. She said that both her father and mother had frequently told her sex was dirty and that she had better not engage in it. She carried the warning and un-earned guilt into adulthood. Helping Lu Ann understand the past provided clues to the present.

A Helpful Framework

One of the valuable aspects of dynamic approaches is that they provide a framework for explaining how people have ar-rived at given stages of life. Part of the genius of Freud's sys-tem is that it makes sense. People can identify with it. Most of us believe that our behaviors and attitudes—indeed the depths of our personalities—have been affected by our early child-hood experiences. The dynamic approaches provide a theory for explaining how this happens: "When I took the time to ex-plore my childhood with a counselor," one man said, "I discov-ered that my fear of women and my guilt over sex harked back to the period in my life when I was strongly drawn to my mother emotionally and was physically pushed away."

It is not necessary to use technical terms or even to under-stand psychodynamic theory to increase our understanding of the effects of childhood on guilt. I have found that helping counselees describe things that happened and *understand feelings* that may have accompanied various events is ade-quate. It is true that some events may have been repressed, pushed out of the individual's awareness. Memories or feel-ings about events will usually resurface as the individual grows in his or her comfort in accepting and dealing with the feelings that are there.

When persons are not aware of their past I sometimes use photo albums or other memorabilia to stir memories and to connect changes in feelings with events. These simple tech-niques allow people to consider their past experiences in a fairly nonthreatening way. Even the person's choice of pic-tures to bring to show me tells me a lot about the person. For example, one counselee chose a happy picture of herself and another one in which her eyes were filled with tears. "Can you see any difference between the girls in these two pic-tures?" I asked her.

When she said no, I said, "Which one is happiest?" She pointed to the younger one. Then I asked her to tell me a story about an event that might have happened that could have made the happy little girl sad. This opened up her awareness of significant things that had happened during her childhood.

Sometimes this approach works, and sometimes it doesn't. A brief walk through childhood with clients can provide valuable insights into the problems of guilt which they may be experiencing. Interestingly, in most cases when people tell stories about their childhood the stories may contain feelings of rejection and guilt. It is very important in listening to such stories to look for the ways in which the parents corrected the child and the kind of respect or disrespect given the child. Labels such as "bad child" or "naughty" often form the basis for unearned guilt in adulthood. I also look for the way affection was given or withheld, as this often forms the basis for either self-acceptance or self-rejection.

Dynamic Approach Suggests the Kind of Experience a Child Needs

In addition to providing plausible explanations of adult feelings and behavior the dynamic approaches also provide suggestions as to the types of healthy experiences a child needs in order to grow into a healthy adult.

Erik Erikson has described eight stages of psychosocial development which a person goes through during a lifetime.[1] He points out that if a person fails to successfully negotiate these stages, he or she will be hindered in future development. The stages are:

1. basic trust versus mistrust
2. autonomy versus shame and doubt
3. initiative versus guilt
4. industry versus inferiority
5. identity versus identity diffusion
6. intimacy versus isolation
7. generativity versus stagnation
8. integrity versus despair

A simple way to remember these eight stages is to ask the question: "What does the person need to experience at each stage?"

Stage One (infancy)—to trust people.

Stage Two (early childhood)—to begin to become autonomous without shame.

Stage Three (childhood)—to take action without guilt.

Stage Four (childhood and adolescence)—to be productive without feeling inferior.

Stage Five (adolescence)—to know who you are as an independent person.

Stage Six (early adulthood)—to be close rather than isolated.

Stage Seven (middle age)—to keep an active mind.

Stage Eight (postretirement)—to feel good about life while growing old.

(The times of life are given as examples of when the stages usually occur.)

While I was talking to Ted about his past he said, "Things were fine until I was about eight. I don't remember anything particular that happened. I just remember the feeling that I couldn't please my parents. I lost confidence in myself. I guess that is when the feelings of guilt really began."

Using Erikson's model we would say that the industry versus inferiority stage was not resolved. Instead of developing confidence in accomplishment (industry), the young man had developed inferiority feelings. These feelings produced unearned guilt. As is so often the case, the problem was compounded by real guilt when the young man began to do unacceptable things in order to get the attention he could not receive through his industriousness.

A careful reading of Erikson's work or the works of other developmental psychologists can provide the counselor with ideas as to the experiences of life a young person can be expected to have.[2] When these experiences have not taken place they may result in feelings of guilt. Once counselees can identify areas where their development was thwarted they can then be led to experiences or new perceptions that will enable them to unhook from that aspect of their past.

Defense Mechanisms

Another contribution of the dynamic approach is the emphasis on defense mechanisms. A defense mechanism is a mental process used by persons to deal with input from their environment, including the environment within their thinking. Defense mechanisms are used to help protect their psychological integrity or to control destructive impulses.

Arthur denied any sexual feelings, and professed to have no interest in sex. This was his defense against a fear of not being able to control himself sexually. He was subconsciously trying to keep his life from being controlled by his sex drive.

I use the concept of balance to explain this to counselees. Our egos or self-concepts can handle being pushed around some by other people or events. We are usually pretty strong and can maintain our balance under most conditions. If, however, a situation should arise that is more than we can take without falling over emotionally, our defenses may arise to keep us balanced.

Natalie was abandoned by her mother at age seven. This was too much for her to take at that time so the defense mechanism of denial came to her rescue. She actually convinced herself that her mother had been needed to take care of other children in an orphanage in Tennessee. "She'll be back," she said, "but right now those other children need her." This defense mechanism kept her balanced and alive at age seven, but she had to deal with it at age seventeen because she began having extreme feelings of guilt and unworthiness. She had kept her feelings suppressed for ten years but they would not be denied during the teenage years.

It behooves the counselor to understand such defense mechanisms as *repression* (excluding impulses and ideas from consciousness); *displacement* (substitutionary replacement of the object or an attitude by another object); *sublimation* (the modification of unacceptable urges so that they become acceptable); or projection (attributing one's own attitudes to others). Most basic textbooks in psychology provide lists of defense mechanisms and illustrations that can help the counselor develop his or her repertoire of things to look for in helping clients understand themselves.

The Inner Power Struggle

Another valuable aspect of the dynamic approach is its emphasis upon the intrapsychic conflicts faced by the counselee. This power struggle within has direct application to problems of guilt which the counselee may be experiencing.

Freud highlighted the conflict between the *id* (the person's baser, pleasure-oriented side), the *super ego* (the code of society or conscience); and the *ego* (the rational, integrated aspect of the mind). Whether one chooses to adopt these concepts or not, it is helpful to realize that all persons who struggle with guilt are aware of the battles between their natural self and the impulses they feel. They also face a battle between the dictates of society or of a significant subculture and their basic urges. Being aware of this battle may help the counselor to assist the counselee in working through the guilt feelings that result.

Another way to look at the internal struggle is to realize that an individual's personality is made up of thoughts, feelings, actions and choices. These four components of personality may be consistent or drastically divergent. Where divergence is present there will usually be feelings of guilt. The highly functioning person (one who has consistent thoughts, feelings, and behaviors) has gone through an integration which unifies the self, minimizes the occurrence of unearned guilt and makes it easier for the person to give and receive forgiveness. Dynamic psychologists point out that there must be a balance among the different aspects of the personality including attitudes, emotions, impulses, and basic satisfactions. Changes in behavior are more likely when they encompass all of these subsystems. In the practical sense, this means that the counselor dare not naively push for change as a way of dealing with guilt without understanding well the effects of change upon the various subsystems operative within a person. The danger is not merely in pushing too hard or too fast; the danger is in pushing in a direction to which the counselee may not be able to respond, and thus increasing the guilt and the internal struggle.

Mabry's counselor was anxious to help him grow so he pushed him into action before either Mabry or the counselor understood the feelings involved. The result was a disaster. Mabry could not follow through on the counselor's suggestions and withdrew from counseling. Shortly thereafter he reverted back to his old patterns of behavior. This could have been avoided if a better balance had been sought by the counselor.

Specific, Relevant Treatment Methods

By suggesting some specific, relevant treatment methods, dynamic theory also contributes to our ability to help persons who suffer with guilt. The concept of using ambiguity has become very useful to me. My tendency has been to want to pin as many things down with the counselee as soon as possible. I believe that I have sometimes pushed so hard to get counselees through their problems that I have made it more difficult for them to resolve their conflicts. But life situations are often ambiguous; some problems of guilt are no-win situations. The counselee may feel guilty regardless of which course of action he or she chooses.

A husband who has had an affair, for example, will feel guilty if he decides to go back to his wife. Such a step will cause his lover to be hurt. Yet he will also feel guilty if he abandons his wife. There is no way out. That is why adultery is such a hurtful sin. If counselees are allowed to struggle with their ambiguity they may better deal with guilt and ultimately make decisions with which they can live. Different people solve problems in different ways and the unstructuredness of the dynamic approaches often provides the opportunity for individual counselees to solve the problems in a way that best fits their personality structures.

Different Methods of Interpretation

Dynamic approaches also point to different methods of interpretation. It is easy to focus upon a purely cognitive approach to interpretation, and ignore the conative aspects—the meaning of things from the counselee's frame of reference. The use of ambiguous techniques such as free association or the recounting of dreams may loosen up the impacted emotions of the counselee and eventually lead to greater self-awareness.

Emma told me about her dreams on numerous occasions.

One day I suggested what a specific dream might mean and it was as though I had flicked on the lights. She began to remember more and understand some of the interrelatedness of the dreams. Suddenly it was safe to remember.

The feelings of the counselees need to be expressed but not in an uncontrolled way. Dynamic techniques often give just enough direction to organize the expression of those feelings. I believe that if feelings about the past are carefully elicited and interpretations are presented to counselees in such a way as not to be overpowering, the process of working through guilt can be greatly expedited. If, however, the interpretations are presented in a somewhat God-like fashion which ignores the meaning of things from the counselees' perspective, guilt may be intensified rather than relieved.

Ross's counselor was the type of person who has a "system" and tries to fit everything into the system. He interpreted some things for Ross, but Ross couldn't understand or could not accept the interpretation. When the counselor insisted he was right, Ross stopped going to counseling. Later Ross had to deal not only with guilt from his past but also with the guilt feelings he had over stopping his counseling. Personally, I doubt that he was the guilty party.

Resistance and Transference

Counseling persons with guilt can also be aided by an awareness of the concepts of *resistance* and *transference* which both come out of the psychodynamic tradition.

Resistance is a technical term that refers specifically to the counselees' attitudes and behavior which are directed toward challenging what others may say about them and toward halting the anxiety that is mounting within. Counselees become resistive when their lives are being read incorrectly by their counselors, and also when the counseling is getting to the point and creating anxiety. For example, Dan began to show up late for his counseling appointments after his counselor suggested that he was angry with his father. He was resistive because the topic created much anxiety for him. Most counselors have recognized that when counselees begin to get better, often they suddenly begin to get worse. This is due to anxiety and resistance. The wise counselor will back off slightly at this point and take another approach that will head back to the same conclusion, but from a different direction.

When Pastor Jim first suggested that Joel's guilt might be related to a fear of closeness with his wife, his idea was met with real resistance. Joel could not handle the anxiety associated with that thought. The pastor might have said, "Why don't you just face up to your fear?" The danger here, however, might have been that Joel would have felt misunderstood and thus less willing to face himself and his problem. By approaching the same issue from a new direction Joel's resistance was weakened. He was eventually able to face his guilty feelings in the context of the fear of closeness he actually experienced. It is good for the counselor to test the resistance of counselees very carefully so as not to drive them into further resistance or even denial.

The concepts of transference and countertransference are also very important considerations in counseling. Transference refers to the counselee's emotional reaction to the counselor. These feelings may be negative, such as fear or hate, or positive, such as feelings of adoration or love. Sometimes the feelings transferred to the counselor are those the counselee actually has toward another person, such as a parent. The concern shown by the counselor in patiently and respectfully dealing with the past will unloose feelings. Whether they are positive or negative and even if they make the counselor feel uncomfortable, they must be addressed. The counselor must allow counselees to deal with those feelings at their own pace.

Marsha said, "When I first started counseling and began to realize all those things about my past, I was angry and I took it out on my counselor. He was my father for a while and I let him have it. Later on, as I worked through some of my feelings, I just wanted him to hold me. Fortunately, he didn't do it, but he didn't reject me either."

Consideration of feelings and the resolution of feelings can be great healers. They dare not be denied. The counselor must realize that feelings are not always based on reality. However, they do show how the counselee sees the world. Counselors need to become comfortable with strong feelings so that the persons whom they counsel can deal with some elements of their past that engender such emotion. Counseling is best served when the counselor is able to describe the feelings rather than get involved in the emotion and take them too seriously. Feelings can be addressed without them controlling the counseling situation.

Sometimes the counselor develops strong feelings toward the counselee. This is called countertransference. Martha, a counselor, said, "I really began to identify with Jane. I felt her pain and her struggle with guilt. Talking with her brought out some of those same feelings in me and there were times when I wanted her to comfort me."

Other counselors have experienced hatred toward their counselees when their life stories have reminded the counselors of their own fearful past. A counselor who feared his own negative feelings toward his wife couldn't deal with his counselee's decision to leave his wife. It brought up too many fears. The counselor became afraid of the possibility that he himself would give in to the same impulse.

The keys to dealing with countertransference are control and accountability. I have supervised many counselors in various stages of training and I have always appreciated it when they have sought advice after recognizing their own feelings of confusion which surfaced in their counseling sessions. It is one thing to feel love toward a counselee. It is a far different matter, however, to keep those feelings alive and to begin to act them out with the other person. This will result in a great wave of guilt for both parties. It is your moral and ethical responsibility not to interact with your counselees for the purpose of meeting your own emotional needs. If you find this happening you must seek guidance and supervision for yourself. And you may need to refer the person to another counselor who can avoid the emotional involvement.

Helping counselees deal with their past often recreates father-daughter or mother-daughter type relationships. These relationships may be therapeutic but they may also result in emotional entanglement. Let the counselor be careful.

Many positive things are to be gained by helping the client work through some of the dynamics of his or her past. If the emotional identifications are controlled, bridges can be built to the present and into the future.

NEGATIVE ASPECTS OF THE DYNAMIC APPROACH

One negative factor characteristic of the dynamic approach is the danger of becoming so involved in interpretation—figuring out what caused certain things to happen—that you never get to the stage of helping the counselee do something about them. Insight doesn't always lead to curative action.

Michael said, "I felt really good for a while. My mind was exploding. I could see all these connections with my past that I had never seen before. After a while, though, I began to get more and more depressed. I guess I realized that I was learning more and more of the problems and wasn't being led to any solutions."

Understanding without resolution is like faith without works. It is dead. One of the major criticisms of the psychoanalytic approach has been that it takes too long and does not always bring about change. I believe this danger can be overcome if the counselor is careful to be sure that the counselees are acting on what they are learning.

I ask counselees, "Now that you see how this may have happened, what kind of things might you do to get to a place of not carrying that guilt any longer?" This leads toward problem-solving which is what counseling is all about.

The Danger of Increased Guilt and Despair

Another drawback of the dynamic approach is the possibility of creating even more guilt and despair as the counselee becomes aware of more and more things that create anxiety. I believe healing must accompany insight, or the counselee may become overwhelmed. I stress the need for closure for the counselee to be able to lay the anxiety to rest. Sometimes I will ask counselees to write or talk to their parents. Sometimes it is necessary to help the counselee forgive or receive forgiveness. Many persons have been helped by the experiences of inner healing.[3] In any case, insight must be coupled with (1) new ways of looking at the situation and (2) emotional resolution.

For Debra, this meant a period of mourning. She had never

accepted her father's death, although he had been dead for years. She was still holding on. After receiving counseling, she went to the gravesite, spent some time weeping and then told her dad that she forgave him, that she loved him, and that she missed him. After that, she was able to begin restructuring her life around the here and now rather than the painful past.

When the past is brought into conscious awareness some counselees ruminate over it and spend large amounts of time introspecting. Paul said, "Sometimes I introspect myself to death." One guideline I have suggested for counselees is that after fifteen or twenty minutes of thinking about a situation they make themselves write down something they are going to do to bring themselves closer to a solution. After they have thought of a positive step they can allow themselves to think more about their hurt. If they aren't thinking of any solutions they are only hurting themselves more and are creating more unearned guilt.

Externalizing the Problem

Another negative aspect of the dynamic approach is the possibility of externalizing the problem. Cheryl said, "When I realized all the things that my dad had done to me I began to blame him for everything. It reached a point where I could rationalize all my failures by pointing the finger at him. It felt really good for a time, because I was released from the burden of self-condemnation I had carried. I came to a point, however, when I had to realize that no matter how badly his abuse had damaged me, I had to take responsibility for many of the choices that were made after the abuse—choices which had kept me crippled."

Once persons are able to accept the responsibility for their choices they are in a position to continue to make the kinds of choices that will lead them out of their guilt.

Donna's mother left her with a sitter and never returned. This had a tremendous impact on her self-esteem and on the development of her social skills during her college years. She hated her mother and hated herself so much that she refused to participate in the friendships extended to her.

One day I said to her, "Your mother was a flake. She left you when you needed her the most. In fact, she didn't even teach you some of the things you need to know about relating to people. My questions, though, are who made you drop out of church where you are getting support? Who made you turn Bill down when he asked you for a date? Who made the decision that you wouldn't look up your father and become adult friends with him?"

After a long period of silence, Donna said, "I guess I really am burying myself, aren't I?"

"Yes," I replied. "What would you like to do about it?"

The tendency to externalize is basic to human defense mechanisms. We blame others because we are not able to handle the self-blame as it arises. When the past is considered and when dynamic causes are discussed it is easy to feel "they made me this way." The skilled counselor will acknowledge the contributions of the past to one's guilt and misery in the present, but at the same time he or she will not allow a counselee to wallow in self-pity.

Failure to Integrate the Past and the Present

Finally, when considering the negative aspects of a dynamic approach we must recognize the danger of failing to integrate past experiences into present dilemmas and future possibilities. Jason said, "The child within me is crying and as an adult I don't know how to act. I'm afraid to live now for fear it will be a recreation of the pain I experienced as a child. I keep myself guilty so that I won't really have to face myself."

At first I didn't know what he meant. Then I realized that he saw himself as two people—an emotionally needy child and a somewhat confused grownup. His "child" was grieving unmet needs and the adult part didn't know how to help. As a means of integration I taught Jason how to care for the emotional needs of the child within on a daily basis. He had to do some things that made him feel better day by day.

"You can't go back to receive support from your father now that he is dead," I reminded him, "but you can decide how you want to treat yourself when the guilt and the sorrows arise."

For Jason the healing process began when he realized that his past was also a part of his present and that he needed to see those needs as manageable now. His father couldn't support him any longer, but he could support himself. As he faced the future he came to realize that it didn't have to look the way it looked through a child's tearful eyes, but that the future could contain the success and optimism which his present adulthood could inject into the picture. He needed the journey through his past in order to better understand his unresolved guilt and other emotions, but he also needed to deal with himself, including his childhood hurts, on a day-by-day basis. Sometimes when he was hurting and couldn't understand why, he would remind himself, *Children have hurts and they hold grudges. Now are you going to just be a child, or are you going to put some adult in there as well?*

Our brief examination of the dynamic approach has underscored the importance of helping counselees deal with the roots of their emotional feelings. Childhood experiences often provide a basis for understanding guilt and other emotions that cannot be explained by just observing present experience. We have highlighted the importance of maintaining the kind of relationship with the counselee that will allow for the loosening of emotions and for greater self-awareness on the part of the counselee. At the same time caution has been given regarding emotional entanglement between the counselor and the counselee. The danger of such entanglement is not unique to the dynamic approaches but may show up in that process because of the emotional impact of dealing with strong feelings. Both counselee and counselor are vulnerable at this point.

In dealing with past material the counselor needs to remain aware of the counselee's tendency to want to change while at the same time sabotaging that change or refusing to integrate new understanding into the ongoing struggle. When anxiety rises too high the wheels of progress will stop. The effective counselor uses the new awareness of the past to help the counselee identify areas of needed growth and then to challenge them and go beyond them to greater freedom from guilt.

CHAPTER TWELVE

BEHAVIORAL AND PROBLEM-SOLVING
APPROACHES TO GUILT

As YOU COUNSEL WITH PEOPLE you will become more and more aware of the ways in which emotional issues such as guilt have behavioral implications for persons. Guilt is often expressed behaviorally by such things as despondency, hostility, or withdrawal from people. The behavior of guilty persons is often inefficient or ineffective. You may also observe that counselees' behavior is greatly affected by the responses they receive from those around them.

Certain patterns of behavior may be encouraged by the positive reactions of people, while other patterns are weakened by the lack of response or by a hostile response. It is highly possible that when people express feelings of guilt and thereby receive a lot of attention they will talk more often about feeling guilty. On the other hand, if expressions of guilt are ignored they will decrease. Does this mean that these people are less guilty? We cannot know for sure. Some would argue that you can only judge by the behavior you observe. In many cases people do use expressions of guilt to get attention. The behavioral approach to guilt suggests that we must examine this and other possibilities.

Although the behavioral approach is often attributed to the research and writings of B. F. Skinner,[1] its origins can be traced back at least thirty years earlier to the work of J. B. Watson. Behaviorists postulated the "law of effect" which states that behaviors that are followed by a positive consequence will increase in frequency, while behaviors that are followed by a neutral or negative consequence will decrease in frequency. This suggests that behavior, even guilt, exists because the person gets a "payoff." The payoff may be related to expressing guilt or to feeling guilt.

Laurie said, "When I feel guilty I talk a lot. This gets me attention for a while. The more I talk, however, people begin to pull away from me, and then I feel I am getting the punishment I deserve." Laurie became aware that she repeated this pattern over and over again. Behaviorists would say that she had learned to feel guilty by first getting attention from others and then receiving from them the punishment she thought she deserved. Both responses increased her feelings of guilt.

LEARNING AND UNLEARNING BEHAVIOR

The behavioral approach stresses the importance of helping counselees learn appropriate or effective behavior and unlearn undesirable or ineffective behavior. Laurie, for example, needed to unlearn the attention-seeking talk associated with her guilt and to unlearn the good feelings she got from interpreting people's withdrawal as punishment or giving her what she deserved.

Learning and unlearning relates to beliefs, attitudes, and emotions, as well as behavior. For example, I have often observed that the beliefs of college students change (are unlearned), not because of new intellectual insight, but because the students are reinforced socially for holding certain beliefs while being punished for holding or, at least, expressing others.

The methods of helping Laurie learn and unlearn behavior can be acquired by studying the behavioral approach. We will limit our discussion here to a few basic principles the counselor can use every day in helping counselees understand and deal with guilt.

Reinforcing Desired Behaviors

Laurie's counselor used a self-reinforcement system to help her learn to show attention to others rather than always seeking attention by her guilt talk. The counselor suggested that Laurie put ten pennies in her pocket. Each time she noticed herself listening or asking questions of another, she was to move a penny to her purse. When all ten pennies had moved to her purse she could treat herself with an ice cream cone, which she loved (which of course cost much more than the ten pennies!).

Although Laurie felt funny at first moving pennies the activity did cause her to think about how she was talking and the eventual reinforcement of ice cream was effective in keeping the new behavior going until a new habit was formed. At the same time the strength of the undesired talk of guilt was lessening due to lack of use. Both results were highly desirable.

Reinforcing desired behaviors can also take place during the counseling session. Norm's counselor wanted him to learn to talk of forgiveness and to review Scriptures related to that subject so the counselor praised Norm when he spoke of forgiveness and when he finished his homework of Scripture review. The praise proved an effective, positive reinforcer and both behaviors increased. This helped Norm get back on track with God. The desired behaviors took the place of some guilt-producing behaviors and Norm's habitual, mental reliving of past guilt which was so destructive.

Reinforcing people for expressed thoughts, attitudes, and behavior which may counteract their guilt can be very effective. The experience of guilt decreases as the thoughts, attitudes, and behaviors are altered. These techniques are especially effective when the person is experiencing unearned guilt or is reliving experiences of guilt for which they have already asked forgiveness.

Breaking Previous Association

Many emotions, including guilt, are learned by association. In much the same way, Pavlov's dog learned to salivate to the sound of a bell when it was presented in association with meat powder.

Consider this example. Bryan, a young man, had stolen from his boss. The boss happened to have a mustache, a seemingly unimportant detail, but, as we will see, a significant detail. Bryan was caught, confessed his wrongdoing and paid back the money. It would seem that the problem was taken care of. Wrong! Bryan began to notice that every time he was in the presence of a man with facial hair his old feelings of guilt would resurface with tremendous power. He had not stolen for two years and was even now on friendly terms with his ex-boss. However, this did not stop this learned guilt from plaguing him. Bryan had to unlearn the guilt by associating with bearded men until he had good feelings and not the negative guilt.

Guilt learned by association can be *un*learned by being in the presence of the guilt-associated stimulus (in Bryan's case, a man with a mustache) without the expected response (being accused). Many, many emotional responses are learned in this way and can only be unlearned when the counselee goes through an extermination process, in this case a pairing of the conditioned guilt-producing stimulus with a positive response. In psychology, this unlearning is known as extinction.

Anna's situation also illustrates the employment of extinction to help with problems of guilt. Her mother always called her by her full name, Anna Marie Swanson, when she was about to scold her. This resulted in Anna's feeling guilty not only when she was scolded, but also when she was called Anna Marie. On one occasion she went to see her pastor because she was depressed after her mother had been to visit her. The wise pastor recognized that the guilt was the result of conditioning so he began to call her Anna Marie as he smiled at her and assured her of God's love and forgiveness. Because the use of her name was no longer paired with scolding, the negative associated feelings were extinguished and the next time the woman's mother came to visit her the response was weak enough that Anna did not suffer from the same guilt feelings.

Many emotional responses such as guilt are learned through conditioning. This produces many of the conditioned emotional responses that may result in feelings of unearned guilt. For example, we feel guilt or failure when we enter a room where in our previous experience guilt or a significant failure may have been experienced. Some people cannot have sex in their own bedroom because of feeling guilt for past failures. Others become fearful of going to church because of guilt experienced there. Many of these problems can be treated by using the process of extinction.

Useful Concepts of Operant Conditioning

Earlier we stated the behavioral principle that behaviors that result in a positive consequence will increase in frequency. This is the major idea in operant conditioning. Consider for a moment what might happen if Dennis tells a friend how guilty he feels and his friend sympathizes with him and goes on and on about it. Dennis is normal and likes attention so it is likely that he will be reinforced by the attention. In this case, even if the friend is able to help him seek and receive forgiveness for his sin, Dennis will still speak often of his guilt because of the response that gets him. Guilt has a payoff for Dennis. It gets him attention like nothing else. The guilt is reinforced by the attention which followed the expression of guilty feelings.

I became aware that Cherry was getting a payoff from telling me about all the bad things she had done and how bad she felt about her actions. She had talked to her pastor about forgiveness so I was sure she understood that she could be forgiven. So, I decided to try an experiment. When she would talk to me about her terrible feelings of guilt I would change the subject or stare off into space. In other words, my response was neutral at best. The more I did this the more she found something else to talk about. I was ignoring the behavior, knowing that if I did so consistently it would go away. I was not giving her a payoff for talking about her guilt. Instead, when she made positive statements about being forgiven or about being used by God I would listen very intently. I wanted to reinforce (give a payoff for) that kind of positive talk. Cherry did not intend to become preoccupied with her guilt, especially after it had been forgiven. However, she was being conditioned to do so by me and others who listened at the wrong times. This was creating severe problems for her and it was hindering the counseling process.

Cherry's friends asked what they could do to help her with her guilt. My response to them was somewhat shocking. "After you are sure she has asked for forgiveness," I said, "then don't talk to her about it."

The Bible seems to indicate that we do a lot of harm by too much talking; Jesus spent a lot of time listening to people. One of the ways Cherry was harming herself was by talking about her guilt and being reinforced by that instead of focusing upon the freedom from guilt that had been received.

If you talk to people about their victories you will reinforce victory. If you talk about the sin and the guilt feelings resulting from that you will reinforce guilt. In that case your counseling is part of the problem, not the solution. Pick your responses carefully. I do not believe in being rude. I believe in hearing people out one or two or even three times. However, when I realize that I am beginning to reinforce behavior that is not good for the counselees or even friends for that matter, I feel I have a responsibility to change the way I relate to them.

My involvement with Darren also illustrates how an awareness of operant learning principles can help in counseling. Each time I would try to help Darren learn some new ways to relate to his wife he would tell me what a miserable failure he had been. When this would happen I would take the pressure off him and drift into a discussion of his guilt. This would reduce his anxiety over having to talk to his wife.

One day I realized I was teaching him to feel guilty rather than what I needed to be teaching him. I was *reinforcing the wrong kinds of behavior,* and I knew I had to reverse the process. The next time I saw him I would not change the subject and I began to use role-playing to reduce his fear of talking to

174

his wife. Through this reversal his anxiety was reduced and he eventually accomplished what he needed to do. Later I confronted him with the way he had used his guilt and I taught him how to stop the process before it kept him from learning the good behaviors he really needed. It took a few more examples and a few more successes before he got the picture clearly. But when he did he was able to deal with the true guilt as it would arise without the intrusion of false guilt as a means of keeping him from doing the fearful but productive things he needed to incorporate into his life.

Behavioral psychologists also stress the importance of *helping the counselees deal with certain behavioral cues,* called discriminative stimuli, which result in the person behaving in an undesirable way because his or her behavior is usually reinforced under the cue condition.

Pastor Brown had a habit of asking his people how they were doing with their struggles with sins. If they said okay he would walk away. If they said not too good he would listen by the hour. His asking the question was a cue or a discriminative stimulus for the person to talk about guilt and failure which was reinforced by careful listening by the pastor. This was discovered as the pastor and I talked over lunch.

He said, "I can't figure it out. My people seem fairly healthy spiritually and yet every time I talk to one of them they just seem to pour out a lot of struggles."

I quizzed him until I guessed what might be happening, and then he decided to experiment by relating differently. The next time he asked the question about struggles with sin and received the answer okay he said, "Sit down and tell me about it." It took a while but before long he was spending more time hearing about victories than wallowing in people's uncertainties or defeats. This allowed him, through listening, to encourage victories rather than defeats. I believe that people say what they think you want to hear. His people were not lying to him. All of us can think of at least one struggle in order to get a few minutes of warm conversation. I believe it is important to reverse these trends by reinforcing the right behavior because people often live what they talk about. If you reinforce talk of guilt and defeat the people who tell you those things will often live in that manner. Similarly, if you discuss victory and joy they will lean in that direction.

Modeling

Another important product of the behavioral approach is *modeling*. People need to observe others dealing with guilt so that they will have a model to follow.

If counselees can see how you confess your sins, receive forgiveness and then go on in your walk with the Lord they will learn from you. Later they may be able to develop an entirely new way of dealing with their guilt. The apostle Paul often challenged people to do what they saw him do (Phil. 4:9).

> Whatever you have learned or received or heard from me, or seen in me—put it into practice. And the God of peace will be with you.

By watching Paul they saw how he was positively reinforced for effective handling of problems such as guilt, and then they would try it for themselves. The result was changed lives better equipped to deal with guilt and other debilitating problems. We need to encourage more modeling in our churches and we need to practice more modeling in our counseling.

There are many reasons why people cannot leave the guilt of their sin. We have discussed some of them, such as the payoff they receive and conditioned emotional responses. One other important reason is that people don't know how to act without their guilt. Successful counselors will model the process themselves and also put counselees in touch with others who can serve as successful models.

USEFUL CONCEPTS FROM A PROBLEM-SOLVING APPROACH

I have observed that many persons who struggle with guilt do not see it as a problem that can be solved. Rather they view it as something that is happening to them which they have no power to control. Sometimes it is very instructive for the counselee if the counselor can outline an approach to dealing with problems and then help the counselee fit his or her guilt struggle into that framework. The simple approach I use has six steps:

1. Define the problem.
2. Decide on some possible solutions.
3. Evaluate the potential good and bad of each solution.
4. Select the best approach.
5. Put the chosen approach into effect.
6. Evaluate the outcome; make changes as necessary.

I used this approach with Bruce who was separated from his wife and had come to me burdened down with guilt. After going over the steps I helped him define the problem. He summarized it as "I really hurt my wife and I need to be able to make it right with her."

Next, we looked for possible ways to solve the problem. He knew he had to talk to her, but he didn't know whether he should also have someone else talk to her, and whether he should call her himself, write to her, or see her personally to discuss the issue. His fear was so great that he wasn't sure he could handle the face-to-face confrontation.

We discussed each of the possible solutions and began to think of the pros and cons of each. This was Step 3. After some time he chose to use a combination of calling and writing (Step 4). He decided to write her a letter telling her what had happened and that he would call to discuss it. After he followed through with his plan (Step 5), he came to see me, to discuss the results (Step 6).

At that point Bruce and I agreed that now he needed to meet with his wife personally in order to further the healing which had begun. During the process of counseling we discovered several other situations that also could be analyzed through such a problem-solving approach as I've suggested. Bruce needed the structure that this particular approach affords. He had tried to deal with his guilt on his own, but until he was able to view it from the perspective of a problem-solving approach he got nowhere.

One valuable side-effect of this approach is its transferability to other situations that may arise. People will constantly have a need to work through guilt and forgiveness with others. If you, as their counselor, teach them a process by which they can solve the immediate concern as well as other situations, you have done them a great service. Bruce's confidence in himself was greatly enhanced by learning this process. It helped him ward off some of the unearned guilt he had experienced when he was floundering, not knowing what to do with his dreadful feelings. The problem-solving approach enabled him to combine spiritual solutions for earned guilt with the emotional and cognitive aids to dealing with unearned guilt. He learned a lot and soon was able to experience a freedom of behavior he had never dreamed of before.

I believe that teaching a problem-solving approach is a very good way to equip the saints. Sometimes the application of biblical truths is hindered by lack of natural skills. Do not assume that people know how to solve problems. Fears and lack of social interaction may have blocked their way to learning and crippled their ability to deal with their own guilt.

NEGATIVE ASPECTS TO THE BEHAVIORAL AND PROBLEM-SOLVING APPROACHES

Like all others, the behavioral approach has some definite limitations.

First of all, *it may not apply to all situations.*

Sometimes it is not possible to analyze the conditioning that may have taken place or that may need to take place. I have also found that sometimes, knowing the things that have been learned and are perpetuating guilt, I cannot always control the associations that have been established or the reinforcers that are present. This is very discouraging at times. When I find myself frustrated in this way I often back up and try again. If I am patient enough I am usually able to help counselees reach a point where they can control their own situations. It is critical not to force all problems into the behavioral mold if they do not fit. On the other hand, this approach should not be overlooked; it is often successful.

Behavioral approaches may also be ineffective if the counselee has a *lack of confidence in the method.* For example, it may be ineffective if the counselee believes that he or she "must get to the root cause." If either the counselor or the counselee doubts the effectiveness of the approach he or she will probably not cooperate carefully enough to understand the behavioral conditions underlying the guilt. Neither will they constructively plan for their elimination. I have found that clients are much more open to a behavioral approach after they have a healthy confidence in the ability of the counselor to understand their guilt. Understanding builds confidence. Confidence builds success.

The counselor also needs to be careful to delay implementation of a behavioral approach until he or she is confident that the use of such an approach will be received by the counselee and will not hinder the counselee's understanding of the confusing, often impacted, feelings involved. It is not satisfactory to solve simple problems behaviorally if this covers up more complex problems or makes them more difficult to assess.

Another drawback of the behavioral approaches that is often encountered is the *inability of the counselor or the counselee to control the reinforcers* or the reinforcing conditions that maintain the learning. If you attempt to intervene behaviorally before you can assume control of the conditions of learning you will probably experience failure and the counselee may experience even more feelings of guilt. Personally, I don't like failure. So, I am careful to think through the counselee's situation to be sure that there is a good chance the behavioral approach will be successful.

Behavioral approaches have also been criticized because of the *nonpermanence* they afford. It is true that if you stop reinforcing a behavior it will cease. If you use a reward system to teach your guilt-ridden counselee a new behavior you must realize that the behavior will stop if the reward is withdrawn. This is not insurmountable. You can teach counselees to reward their own behavior or you can teach others who are around them to reward them. The point is: this issue must be given special attention. We cannot assume that just because a behavior has been learned that it will automatically be maintained.

After months of not feeling guilty around women, Kurt was yelled at and cursed by a female where he worked. This resulted in renewed fear of women and renewed guilt in their presence.

This illustrates what often happens with emotional responses such as guilt that have previously been stopped. If the original conditions under which they were learned are repeated they will reoccur and usually very quickly. This may account for people suddenly beginning to feel guilty over their past when it has not bothered them for months. They may have begun to have flashbacks or the old situation in which the guilt was originally learned may have reoccurred.

These situations are very complex and require patience to figure out. They need not hinder the application of the behavioral approach, but they may require that the counselor take the counselee back through the learning process again so that the desired thoughts, feelings, or behavior can be reestablished.

A behavioral approach may also be counterproductive when the counselee suffers from other *pathological conditions* which may serve to block the learning process. This is especially true if the counseling is being conducted in a setting in which the counselor has little or no control over the client.

Floyd wanted to learn some new responses to his guilt and his counselor could see how that might be accomplished. The plan failed, however, because Floyd was a very controlling person and had used his fears as a means of controlling others. His need to control was stronger than his need to be free from the fears, so the plan was sabotaged. I have also observed counselees getting reinforcement from other sources when the major reinforcers for their unearned guilt were controlled.

Occasionally counselees who suffer from thought disorders will not respond to new conditioning because of their overall level of confusion. Although behavioral principles have been shown to be effective with a wide range of mental problems their effectiveness may vary depending on the nature of the problem being attacked. If the principles are not working I advise discontinuing them. It does no good to force them upon a confused mind.

Even though we have discussed several drawbacks to the behavioral approaches they still have much to offer and can often be used effectively with other approaches. They do, however, require precise application and should not be tried if they are not given enough attention to make them effective. When in doubt seek the advice of someone who is knowledgeable in this area.

A word of caution must also be given regarding the use of the problem-solving approach. It is sometimes criticized by clients who believe they already have the skills automatically and therefore are being asked to waste their time. I have dealt with this concern by asking, "How have you tried to solve this problem?" or, "What approaches have you used?" before I introduce the formal approach. This has often been successful in breaking down counselees' resistance and in increasing their interest in a formal approach.

We must also recognize that where guilt is involved not all situations have a simple solution. Some are what Paul Welter calls dilemmas. He writes:

> There is, then, a considerable difference between having a *problem* and being in a *predicament*. The term "problem," whether applied to a mathematical problem or a personal problem, implies there is a solution. All that is needed is to come up with the correct insight or enough knowledge and apply this solution to the problem. . . . A predicament, on the other hand, suggests a difficult situation offering *no* satisfactory solution.[2]

When people are faced with predicaments that are not solved the feelings of guilt will rise even higher. Counselors need to exercise discernment and point out to counselees that they might experience even more guilt if they expect to be able to treat a predicament in the same way they do a problem. The consequences of sin are often a *predicament,* and counselees must be helped to see them that way if further guilt is to be avoided.

Phil, for example, had stolen money from his company and had lost his job. As a result he was unable to pay his bills and was having difficulty finding a new job. The effects of Phil's sin were ongoing and he could not protect some of the people he loved who were getting hurt. The best he could hope for was forgiveness by God and his family and the grace to avoid any further transgressions. He needed a chance to express his feelings and to grieve over his sin. Phil, like many counselees, was involved in a process of being freed from guilt. His greatest need was for emotional support, and that does not require the application of any problem-solving techniques. The problem-solving approach was applicable to part of his situation, but not all of it.

Finally, the problem-solving approach may be deficient if a *proper analysis of the guilt is not made.* As was stated earlier, unearned guilt may be very complex and the origins of it may take some time to uncover. When this is the case the counselor should wait patiently until the usefulness of applying the problem-solving approach can be clearly seen. It is helpful to look at all counseling situations from a problem-solving perspective, however. Not all situations lend themselves quickly to this approach.

This brief encounter with behavioral and problem-solving approaches should stimulate the counselor to look at the problems of guilt from as broad a perspective as possible. It is intended to supplement the methods described earlier—that deal with feelings and thoughts—by dealing with behaviors and choices which may solve the problems. Combined, they serve to cover the broad spectrum of human personality.

PART THREE

PREVENTING GUILT

CHAPTER THIRTEEN

PRACTICAL WAYS TO PREVENT GUILT

THE VERY THOUGHT OF PREVENTING GUILT may be troublesome to some readers. After all, conviction of sin is a function of the Holy Spirit and guilt is often associated with conversion and recommitment to Christ. Few would argue that true guilt must not be prevented, but that it must be met with confession and forgiveness. Preventing true guilt would result in the absence of redemption and healing.

There is a need, however, for the prevention of perpetual or chronic guilt which lingers and immobilizes the person long after the records in heaven have been cleared. There is also a need to help people deal with the various types of un-earned guilt discussed in chapter 5. People often cannot sort out feelings on their own. They must be helped to recognize that not all feelings of remorse come as the result of sin and conviction by the Holy Spirit. Some feelings of guilt are better attributed to psychological rather than spiritual causes. *The psychologically related guilt which has no purpose in God's plan should be prevented whenever possible.*

Any approach to human concerns that ignores the importance of prevention is a firefighting technique at best. We cannot afford to do individually those things that can be accomplished in either large or small groups. On the other hand, the experiences we offer to people must be carefully directed to the concerns of the individuals. We have to meet them where they are. This requires that we know about problems and that we understand people. Understanding the backgrounds and value systems of counselees is critical in both counseling and prevention.

ELEMENTS OF PREVENTION

The church is in a unique position to help with prevention of unearned and unnecessary guilt because people expect that the church should speak authoritatively about guilt. Unfortunately, the message of Scripture regarding guilt and forgiveness is not always clearly presented and/or accurately received. Through good, biblically based preaching, sensitive teaching, and the development of restorative and growth-oriented fellowship groups a major impact can be made.

Pitfalls to Be Avoided

There are certain things to be avoided and other important applications to be considered. We will consider three of each.

First, preaching and teaching need to *avoid motivation by guilt*. Even though this problem was discussed in chapter 6 it must be reemphasized here. Making people feel bad doesn't result in their doing good. Statements such as "if you love God, you will . . ." are not very helpful. They combine elements that may not be related. You may love God dearly and still not volunteer to attend church every time the doors are open. In like manner, you may love God and still sin. The preventive emphasis needs to be upon positive action the hearer can take, not on negative behaviors or things that should create guilt. Accusatory preaching and teaching is not always true. It often represents the biases of the teacher and not the truth of Scripture.

God wants people to change, not because he will feel bad if they don't, but because it is in their own best interest to change. Jesus did not tell Peter over and over again about his faults and failures. He said, "Feed my sheep." He acknowledged Peter's repentance and love.

Another pitfall to be avoided if one's preaching and teaching is to have a preventive effect is *trying to heal people by injunction.* I have found statements such as "all you have to do is trust God" to not be very helpful. In most cases if people knew how to trust God they would have. When they are enjoined to do something for which they do not have the skills, unearned guilt will result. We need to follow the emphasis of Scripture to equip the saints.

And let us consider how we may spur one another on toward love and good deeds. Let us not give up meeting together, as some are in the habit of doing, but let us encourage one another—and all the more as you see the Day approaching. (Heb. 10:24, 25)

This Scripture emphasizes three things that relate to prevention: spurring toward love and good deeds, meeting together, and encouragement.

Until I became a horse owner and watched a skillful trainer at work I never fully understood this passage. I thought spurs were used to punish or to goad, which is the impression one would get from watching a rodeo. What is the purpose of the spurs? My trainer says it's guidance. They are used to signal to the horse which way to go. If used punitively the horse will become confused or rebel. The trainer shows the horse what to do and then signals by the use of spurs when it is time to do it. This is a perfect example of the type of behavior that prevents guilt. Instruct in the desired behavior and signal in that direction—instruct and guide.

Meeting with people is also a great tool of prevention. As

people interact they can be helped to stay on target, avoid sin, and keep their past sins in proper perspective.

Ned's friend said, "You told us last week that that sin had been forgiven. Is there any reason you are still harping on it?" Ned got the picture and an unnecessary journey into guilt was diverted.

Encouragement is essential to prevention. Human beings have a tremendous capacity to self-destruct if not encouraged. The writer of Hebrews stresses, remember, remember, remember. Remember what God has done. That's encouragement. Remember that your sins have been forgiven. Remember to avoid behavior and thoughts that will produce sin and guilt.

Neal told his friend, "You owe it to yourself to have a clear conscience for a while." This was certainly an ounce of prevention, well applied.

Lest I violate my own principle I need to combine my own injunction with some instruction. Let's use the example of trusting God.

Chuck said, "I don't know how many times I have been told to trust God, but I fail every time. I guess I'm either too bad or too stupid to know what that means."

After assuring him that I did not believe either evil or stupidity to be the problem, I said, "Let's find some ways that you can begin to trust God. What are some small steps you could take that would make you feel that you were trusting God?" Chuck's mind went blank at first and I had to work to keep his thinking on the question. It seemed hopeless at times. Finally he said, "I guess one thing I could do is talk to my dad. I have never thought of that before, but I would really have to trust God for the power to do that."

After a time of musing Chuck asked, "Doesn't God have to do something great in me before I can trust?" He had made the error of thinking that trusting God is always passive. He had to take some active steps before he could trust God by patiently waiting. Once he entertained an idea (talking to his dad) as a starting place, the process of learning to trust was underway.

I have found that pastors and teachers often spend too much time *telling* and not enough time *helping* people discover those practical first steps. We often assume that if people do not act it is because of a bad attitude or a lack of spirituality. On the contrary, I believe many are suffering badly from a lack of models to follow. We need people in positions of authority not only to enjoin us to change but to actually show us how one goes about exercising faith, receiving forgiveness, or accepting love. Injunctions tell us *what* but they do not tell us *how*. I am not arguing against teaching principles but I am arguing that the most effective teaching, especially as it relates to the prevention of guilt, is teaching that shows as well as tells.

> Command and teach these things. Don't let anyone look down on you because you are young, but *set an example* for the believers in speech, in life, in love, in faith and in purity. (1 Tim. 4:11, 12)

Closely related to the problem of trying to heal by injunction is the method of *providing simple solutions*. I never assume that my counselee's problems are easy to solve. In fact, I have a strong belief that if they were simple the counselee would have solved them already. Caution must be taken not to create another layer of guilt by implying that the solutions are so apparent that if the counselee was adequate at all he or she would have known. Prevention is best served, I think, by teaching a process of solving problems as discussed in chapter 12. Unearned guilt is prevented when counselees feel that they have acquired some tools.

When solutions to human problems are presented publicly as very simple or simplistic ("just trust Jesus" or "all you have to do is talk to the person"), they are often ignored. The listener knows down deep that his or her attempts to follow such advice will not be any more successful than they were the last time. When this happens they become immobilized and guilt resulting from lack of action will arise. At this point they usually drop out of church or counseling. The instructor's credibility is also weakened because the person believes that the counselor or instructor does not really understand. If prevention is to be served when specific solutions are given they must be accompanied by step-by-step ways of carrying them out and a willingness on the part of the instructor to support the person as the solutions are applied.

Paul Welter,[1] as I have pointed out, makes the important distinction between a problem and a predicament. He discusses how problems have a solution so advice is usually helpful, while predicaments have no easy or satisfactory solution so advice is usually not helpful. Therefore, one needs to know what the situation is before giving advice.

There are times when people need to be instructed in a declarative manner if guilt is going to be stopped. Here is an example.

"John, have you ever asked God to forgive you for what you did? Have you told him you were wrong?"

"No," he replied. "I think I'm afraid to do so."

After discussing his fears I said, "John, I think you need to ask God to forgive you right now. Until you have asked for forgiveness you can't know how you will feel."

Both asking for forgiveness and forgiving others seem very simple but they are not. They involve fears and other emotional blocks that the counselee may not understand. When solutions or action steps are suggested, enough support must be provided to enable the counselee to follow through.

Predicaments can also be addressed preventively. Susan was seventeen when her parents started the process of divorce. She was confused, hurt, angry, and frantically searching for some solution. Her youth pastor was most helpful through what he said both publicly and privately. Before Susan even knew there was a problem between her mom and dad she had heard him speak on the topic: "You can't be responsible for your parents." She remembered this talk when she needed it the most. Privately, the youth pastor listened to her frustration and anger and guided her into the "art" of being angry and sinning not. Guilt was prevented. Susan still felt a lot of pain and had to spend some time grieving, but at least she was spared the added layer of pain caused by unearned guilt over something outside of her influence or control.

Avoiding motivation by guilt, not trying to heal by injunction, and refusing to toss out simple solutions will pave the way for true prevention of guilt. My father's advice to me as I was growing up is applicable precisely at this point. "Son," he would say, "be careful what you say. Someone might just be listening to you."

Positive Steps Toward Prevention

Prevention is often served by *incisive action*. Just as death by cancer may be prevented by regular attention to danger signs, guilt may be avoided by taking action related to sin or related to the various sources of unearned guilt.

David had not been able to talk to his father about the way he reacted to some of his dad's criticism. David's pastor finally said, "You have put this off long enough. If you can't talk to your dad alone I will go with you." This was incisive action. David was pushed off the fence. Later he told the pastor, "You will never know how much better I feel. It's like a big weight has been taken off my chest."

I often promote action by asking two questions: "What would you like to see happen in this situation?" and "What action do you feel you need to take right now to get the ball rolling?" These questions are as appropriate from the pulpit or the lectern as they are from the counselor's chair. When people are unable to answer questions of this type it may mean that no one has helped them analyze the source of their guilt. Thus they are confused and immobilized.

In response to my first question, Sharon said, "I don't know, I just know I want to feel better." Until we determined whether her guilt was earned or unearned it was hard to know what action was indicated for her to reach her goal. The guilt was resolved quickly after it was understood and future guilt was prevented as she realized that in cases of unearned guilt the feelings do not always follow immediately on the heels of the action. It takes time for our emotions to assimilate the facts, even when appropriate action has been taken.

A second positive prevention step is directing people to *choose right* (nonguilt-producing) *behavior*. People often feel guilty because they are not living up to who they believe God has made them to be. When people take positive action, guilt subsides. When they ponder positive steps but do not take them, guilt builds. Remember—instruct and guide. Push or spur a little as needed.

My wife Sandy does this so well. "Shirley," she said, "you have told me you need to spend some positive time with your daughter. When do you have that scheduled for this week?"

Shirley answered, "I don't."

After a time they agreed that Sandy would hold Shirley accountable to do the positive things she needed to do with her daughter, and Shirley would hold Sandy accountable for some growth steps she wanted to take in her life. Through their mutual support they were both able to take the kind of action that made each of them feel she was making progress. Thus feelings of guilt were avoided.

Sometimes there is a narrow line between challenging people to be all they can be and motivation by guilt. I believe the difference is seen in this manner. Challenging people to be all they can be says, "You need to do it and I am willing to help equip you so you can." Motivation by guilt says, "If you are a true Christian you will." People who motivate by guilt may fail to offer to help equip the person. That approach is not very helpful.

It is a wonderful thing to have people believe in you and challenge you to remember that the power of God resides within you. However, it is a frightening thing to have people demand performance from you without believing in you, equipping you, or pointing out the great power of God. If we are going to prevent unnecessary guilt and help people leave the earned guilt of their past in pursuit of new possibilities of worship and service, we need to give more careful attention to this matter.

Another positive prevention step, *helping people leave the past behind,* is illustrated in this way:

Mark: I feel terrible—I lied to my father and I feel like he will never trust me again.

Pastor Johnson: Tell me what has happened since the lie.

Mark: Well, I felt guilty as soon as I realized that I had done it. I'm not a very good liar anyway. I told my dad I was sorry and I confessed it to God.

Pastor: What did each of them say?

Mark: What do you mean?

Pastor: How did your dad respond and how did God respond?

Mark: Well, Dad was real neat about it. He told me he was disappointed that I had lied but he was proud that I was man enough to come to him with the truth.

Pastor: Has he forgiven you?

Mark: He said he did.

Pastor: Does he tell lies?

Mark: I sure don't think so.

Pastor: Okay! What about it? Has he forgiven you or not?

Mark: (with a smile) He has, hasn't he? That's good!

Pastor: Let's talk about God then. What did he say?

Mark: I wish I knew. I know that lying is breaking one of the Ten Commandments. I've always been afraid that if I broke one of them I would just go crazy and do everything bad.

Pastor: You did tell me though that you asked God to forgive you? (Mark nodded.) Well, did he do it or not? (Mark looked confused and sat silently.) Can you think of any Scripture that might answer that for you?

Mark: I know 1 John 1:9. It says he is faithful and forgives when we confess things to him.

Pastor: Maybe that's not true! (Now Mark really looked puzzled. Pastor Johnson continued.) If you have asked him to forgive you and still feel terrible, maybe God has lied.

Mark: You're putting me on, aren't you? You know good and well the problem isn't God. It's me.

Pastor: Okay, so you believe God. Where is the problem then? Somewhere you are believing a lie.

Mark: What lie is that?

Pastor: The lie that you should feel terrible.

Mark: I guess that's the way I feel.

Pastor: Does that make it true? (Mark shook his head.)

Pastor: Feelings are real but they are not always true. I believe God wants you to feel good—good about him and good about yourself because your sins have been forgiven. (Unless, of course, God has been lying to you.) I have always found it to be a wonderful thing that God loves me so much he forgives me. How can I help you to focus on that for a while?

Mark: You already have. I need to focus on the fact that God has forgiven me.

Pastor: Okay, then we have one more thing to finish. You said your dad will never trust you again. How did he say that to you? Was he angry?

Mark: No, he wasn't angry. He didn't even yell.

Pastor: What did he say?

Mark: He said, "Son, I forgive you."

Pastor: He didn't mean it though.

Mark: (Looking almost annoyed) Of course he meant it!

Pastor: He meant it but he neglected to tell you that he will never trust you again. That was kind of mean!

Mark: Okay! Okay! I get the message. He didn't say he could never trust me again. I said that to myself.

Pastor: There you go lying again. I don't believe that you will never be trustworthy again, do you?

Mark: No. But lying to Dad came too easily; I guess I was afraid that I would keep doing it.

Pastor: Have you?

Mark: No.

Pastor: Then maybe you can trust yourself. Once again, let's look at what is true in this situation. The problem doesn't seem to be in your confidence in your dad's ability to trust you, but in *your* ability to trust you. You are emotionally down on yourself right now so you need to be extra careful to emphasize what you believe to be true, not just what your feelings are telling you.

Mark got the point and then Pastor Johnson was able to lead him to some new steps of freedom.

Pastor: Do you suppose God understands your weakness at this point?

Mark: Yes.

Pastor: Then let's use this as an opportunity to seek his help and not just as an opportunity to continue to punish yourself for what you have done.

This type of incident is repeated over and over again in my office. Unnecessary guilt will be acquired or maintained unless people are helped to a step-by-step unhooking from some of the feelings which are a carryover from their sin. Their beliefs and feelings which are not founded on true observations of the situation or of Scripture must be challenged. If this does not take place then guilt runs wild—not true guilt based on sin, but unearned guilt that is based upon failure to correctly analyze the situation. Guilt can be prevented when counseling is focused upon reality, and not upon the intellectual or emotional ideas of the client. Prevention can also take place when preaching and teaching help people stay focused on the freeing message of forgiveness, not the horribleness of sin.

Finally, positive steps toward the prevention of guilt are taken when there is *affirmation of victories.*

"Joyce," I said, "it's time for a celebration. You have made some real progress. I want to review some of these steps with you and thank God for each one." Joyce was reluctant at first because she had been trained by her parents to be shy about success. Soon, however, the thoughts began to come and she began to smile and relate her successes to me. We thanked God after each one and tears of joy began to flow.

I believe that God loves celebrations and that they are a great vehicle for healing and for the prevention of guilt. On occasion I have led groups of people through such a celebration at the completion of a conference or a church service. I believe God rejoices and is praised and people remember their victories, not their guilt.

The reader will develop his or her own positive steps of prevention. The four presented—incisive action, directed choices, leaving the past behind and celebration of victories—will help get the process started.

COMMON AVENUES FOR PREVENTION

When you consider the many avenues that may be used to prevent guilt the most obvious is *good, sound biblical preaching.* It is the truth that sets people free from guilt. A caution must be sounded, however. Sometimes preaching does not focus on the positive proclamation of the gospel but upon pet peeves and gimmicks. The message of forgiveness and redemption sets people free from sin and guilt. The message must be presented loudly and clearly.

The story of Mark and his pastor told in the preceding paragraphs emphasizes another important aspect of prevention—*positive teaching*. Pastor Johnson was caring, but tough. He used his discernment to help Mark and he taught Mark to discern for himself. One-on-one teaching or discipling is vital if people are to be helped to establish their lives on Scripture and correct observations of God's ways rather than their own feelings of despair. In one sense, counseling can be defined as good one-on-one teaching. There was nothing magical about what Pastor Johnson accomplished—it was just careful hard work that led to prevention of further guilt and suffering for Mark.

Large group teaching can also be a means of preventing guilt. Scriptures related to guilt need to be carefully studied and applied to the lives of students. False views or distorted views of God need to be examined in view of their implications for both earned and unearned guilt. In all cases, the teaching situation must provide the opportunity for students to discover which beliefs or feelings about guilt are based upon Scripture and which may be based upon feelings, extrabiblical church tradition or even non-Christian ideas. If this is to be accomplished, an atmosphere for learning must be created which allows people to ask questions and to interact with other believers who are interested in knowing the truth and being set free by it.

In recent years the small group movement has become very popular within church circles. I believe a good *small group* offers a tremendous resource for dealing with and preventing guilt.

In a small group people can be honest. They can learn to express themselves and can hold one another accountable. They can challenge each other's misconceptions. These elements are often lacking in the large group setting. Small groups should function as families, offering forgiveness, support, and opportunities to develop self-understanding.

Dan said, "I began to get straightened out when I was able to open up to my fellowship group." This can and will take place when the emphasis is upon vulnerability and growth, not on perfection as a condition for membership. A perfectionistic emphasis will lead to further guilt, while an emphasis upon acceptance and growth will lead to forgiveness and the prevention of further guilt.

Finally, a discussion of prevention would be incomplete without a statement on the importance of *friendship*. I can hide from many people and cause others to believe what I want them to believe about me, but I can't do this with my true friends. They know me and often assist me to see my life more realistically. This helps me deal with guilt and stay mentally healthy. A friend will tell me when I am lying to myself. A true friend will tell me when I am flirting with evil and he or she will not let me wallow in the guilt of past sin that has been forgiven. I believe that friendships both inside and outside the family are the greatest mental health resources we have. Healthy churches emphasize friendships which result in even greater degrees of health among the members.

Counseling concerning guilt will not be adequate or complete until the elements of prevention are used and the avenues of prevention are followed. I would rather help people avoid guilt than help them deal with the pain it causes.

CHAPTER FOURTEEN

AVOIDING COUNSELOR GUILT

WHEN MY TYPIST, GAIL, who is also a skilled lay counselor, finished the first draft of this manuscript she pushed away from the typewriter and said, "Whew, I feel guilty!" When I asked for an explanation she said, "Even though I have counseled a lot I realized as I typed that I make a lot of mistakes in counseling. I imagine there have been times when I made the problems worse rather than better." I encouraged Gail to consider the possible mistakes but not to get so caught up in them that she failed to recognize the many ways God had used her. I encouraged her to avoid the trap of counselor guilt. She, like many people I have supervised, wants so much to do everything right that she is in danger of becoming encumbered with her own guilt and losing the joy of using the gifts God has given her.

Here are some principles that Gail and others like her need to remember in order to avoid the guilt trap.

Remember that *you do not have to be perfect to be effective.* I am always amazed at how God takes some of my errors and turns them into learning for the counselee.

I wasn't listening carefully enough to Rose and said something that revealed my lack of understanding. Noticing her countenance change, I began to search for the cause of the misunderstanding. The process took several minutes, but when it was over I did understand and was able to apologize to her. As a result she felt valued again and we had a new and even stronger base from which to work. Later she said half jokingly, "I didn't know about you for a while. I didn't know whether you had given up on listening to me or whether I should give up on you." The quality of the interaction was less than perfect but it had turned out okay because we both worked at correcting the mistake.

Remember that *change comes slowly.* Therefore, you would have to repeat most mistakes several times in order to create negative change. The errors that counselors make are taken seriously by counselees but they do not often result in immediate negative consequences. Sometimes counselees will go back over the same territory in essence to give the counselor a second chance. When a counselee repeats a statement or goes back over a topic, monitor your response carefully. Ask yourself whether you may be misunderstanding or whether your earlier response may have created confusion or been damaging to the counseling relationship. When you spot what may have been an error do not hesitate to go back to correct it.

"Russ," I said, "when I told you that you needed to trust God more I don't think I was being very helpful. I do believe that you trust God and I want to help you grow to trust him even more. Forgive me if I added to your guilt trip." Russ's face became less tense and I knew that we were back on the right track. I hadn't continued to repeat the mistake so negative change was avoided.

Remember that *counselees are often loving and tolerant of counselor error.* Kim said, "I put up with a lot from you. If you didn't help me so much I probably wouldn't stand for all your 'guff.'"

When you counsel people you will not always be at your best—but you will still care. (If you don't, then please don't counsel.) This caring means a lot to your counselees and they will care back. When counselees are loving and tolerant, thank them for it. When they are overly sensitive to your mistakes, apologize and ask for their forgiveness. Rarely will they refuse to give it.

This give and take between counselors and counselees will serve as a model that may help counselees to know how better to relate in the world in which they live. Kim said, "You have taught me a lot about relating by the way you relate to me. Neither of us has to pretend to be perfect. We make mistakes but we don't have to feel guilty. I am growing a lot."

Remember that *mistakes can be reversed.* Occasionally you will work with a person for some time and will realize that you have not been getting anywhere. When this type of thing happens it usually means that you are on the wrong track. You may have made a mistake.

One counselee was making good progress for several weeks and then things began to change until finally he stopped coming altogether. I needed to know why. After a telephone call I realized that I was laboring under some false assumptions about his guilt. Further, I realized he did not have confidence in me to help him because of the error. I invited him to come in for a free "let's see if we can straighten this thing out" session. He did so and as a result he had renewed confidence in me and I had a greater appreciation for him. The mistake was rectified and after a short time he was able to accomplish his goals for counseling. The mistake was reversed because I was not satisfied just to feel guilty but pursued until I got to the source of the problem. I felt better and he felt better. Pursuing him also gave him a greater sense of worth because he realized that I cared too much for him to just let him drift off without further contact.

Finally, remember that *mistakes are usually not serious as long as you remain teachable.* When I admit a mistake and seek ways of dealing with it I will probably not damage my counselee. The worst that usually happens is a slowing down of the healing process.

On the other hand, if I let my pride get in the way and either deny my error or blame it on my counselee I will become a part of the problem rather than part of the solution. Denial of responsibility for your own behavior can be devastating. But accepting responsibility can bring splendid results. Notice the contrast in the following two situations.

Mitch said, "I don't think you understand. . . ."

The counselor responded, "No, it is you who don't understand. When are you going to listen to me?"

The result was obvious: more guilt for Mitch, greater distance between the counselee and the counselor.

Richard said, "I don't think you understand. . . ."

The counselor responded, "I may have missed something. Let's go through this once more. I need to see it through your eyes." The result: clarification of communication and a greater working relationship between counselor and counselee. The mistake was avoided because the counselor was willing to learn.

Counseling with persons who suffer with guilt is both a great privilege and a great responsibility. You will do your best work as a counselor when you concentrate on your strengths rather than punishing yourself for your weaknesses. The more relaxed you can be about your own counseling performance the more likely you are to meet the needs of your counselees.

As I counsel I often pray, "Lord help me to be attentive, compassionate, and willing to learn from you and this counselee. On the other hand, God, help me to be clear and concise so that my counselee can learn from you and me as well." A positive attitude helps avoid numerous errors and a great deal of guilt. Guilt! Who needs it?

BIBLIOGRAPHY

Helpful books not quoted in the foregoing material.

Drakeford, John W., *Integrity Therapy*, (Nashville, Broadman Press, 1967).

Justice, William G., *Guilt and Forgiveness:* How God Can Help You Feel Good About Yourself, (Grand Rapids, Mich.: Baker, 1980).

Justice, William G., *Guilt, the Source and the Solution*, (Wheaton, Ill.: Tyndale House, 1981).

Kinzer, Mark, *Living with a Clear Conscience:* A Christian Strategy for Overcoming Guilt and Self-Condemnation, (Ann Arbor, Mich.: Servant Books, 1982).

Narramore, Bruce, *No Condemnation*, (Grand Rapids, Mich.: Zondervan, 1984).

Oden, Thomas C., *Guilt Free*, (Nashville: Abingdon Press, 1980).

Stein, Edward V., *Guilt: Theory and Therapy*, (Philadelphia: The Westminster Press, 1968).

NOTES

Chapter 1 The Challenges of Counseling for Guilt

1. David Augsburger, *The Freedom of Forgiveness* (Chicago: Moody Press, 1970), 75.

Chapter 2 Biblical Perspectives on Guilt

1. Earl D. Wilson, *The Discovered Self* (Downers Grove, Ill.: InterVarsity Press, 1985).

Chapter 3 Psychological Perspectives on Guilt

1. Karl Menninger, *Whatever Became of Sin?* (New York: Hawthorn Books, 1973), 218.
2. Nancy Anne Smith, *Winter Past* (Downers Grove, Ill.: InterVarsity Press, 1977), 20–21.
3. See David Belgum in *Guilt: Where Religion and Psychology Meet* (Minneapolis: Augsburg, 1970).

Chapter 4 The Need for an Integrative Approach to Guilt

1. Bruce Narramore, *You're Someone Special* (Grand Rapids, Mich.: Zondervan, 1978), 144.
2. See David Stoop, *Self-talk: Key to Personal Growth* (Old Tappan, N.J.: Fleming H. Revell, 1982); Paul Hauck, *Overcoming Frustration and Anger* (Philadelphia: The Westminster Press, 1975); Milton Loyden, *Escaping the Hostility Trap* (Englewood Cliffs, N.J.: Prentice-Hall, 1977); Lloyd J. Ogilvie, *Making Stress Work for You* (Waco, Tex.: Word, 1984).

Chapter 5 Earned and Unearned Guilt

1. Karen Horney, *The Neurotic Personality of Our Time* (New York: W. W. Norton and Co., 1937), 230–231.
2. Andrew D. Lester, *Coping With Your Anger: A Christian Guide* (Philadelphia: The Westminster Press, 1983), 28.

Chapter 6 The Problem of Motivation by Guilt

1. David Augsburger, *The Freedom of Forgiveness* (Chicago: Moody Press, 1970), 76.
2. Paul Tournier, *Guilt and Grace* (New York: Harper and Row, 1962), 18.
3. Bruce Narramore, *You're Someone Special*, 145.
4. Bruce Narramore and Bill Counts, *Freedom from Guilt* (Eugene, Ore.: Harvest House, 1974), 26.

Chapter 7 Love and Guilt

1. C. S. Lewis, *The Four Loves* (New York: Harcourt, Brace and Jovanovich, 1960), 166.
2. John Powell, *Unconditional Love* (Niles, Ill.: Argus Communications, 1978), 56.
3. Paul Welter, *How to Help a Friend* (Wheaton, Ill.: Tyndale House, 1978), 38.
4. Bruce Narramore, *You're Someone Special*, 121.

Chapter 8 Relationships and Guilt

1. Howard Halpern, *Cutting Loose* (New York: Bantam Books, 1976), 1–2.
2. Dorthea McArthur, *The Birth of a Child in Adulthood*, unpublished manuscript, 1986.
3. Gary Inrig, *Quality Friendship* (Chicago: Moody Press, 1981, 60–61.
4. Ibid, 57–58.
5. Earl D. Wilson, *Loving Enough to Care* (Portland, Ore.: Multnomah Press, 1984), 83.
6. Earl D. Wilson, *A Silence to be Broken* (Portland, Ore.: Multnomah Press, 1986). For further study in the subject of spousal, child, and elder abuse, see Volume 6 in the Resources for Christian Counseling series, *Counseling for Family Violence and Abuse* by Grant L. Martin, published by Word, Inc., 1987.

Chapter 9 Cognitive Approaches to Guilt

1. See Albert Ellis and Russell Grieger, *A Handbook of Rational Emotive Therapy* (New York: Springer, 1977).
2. Pamela E. Butler, *Talking to Yourself* (Harper and Row, 1981), 81.
3. Lawrence Crabb, *Effective Biblical Counseling* (Grand Rapids, Mich.: Zondervan, 1977), 160.

Chapter 10 Self-Discovery Approaches to Guilt

1. C. H. Patterson, *Theories of Counseling and Psychotherapy*, 2nd ed. (New York: Harper and Row, 1973), 395.

Chapter 11 Dynamic Approaches to Guilt

1. Erik H. Erikson, *Identity, Youth and Crisis* (New York: W. W. Norton and Co., 1968).
2. See David Elkind, *The Hurried Child* (Reading, Mass.: Addison-Wesley, 1981) and *All Grown Up and No Place to Go* (Reading, Mass.: Addison-Wesley, 1984); also, Rolf E. Muus, *Theories of Adolescence*, 3rd ed. (New York: Random House, 1975).